Cover Design Description

The book cover was designed by a friend of mine who, when praying about my book, received a revelation from God regarding the design for the front and back covers.

On the front is depicted the living water flowing from heaven to earth and becoming narrower to illustrate the narrow path leading to eternal life.

The back cover is symbolic of Jesus on the Cross. This design depicts living water descending from heaven and penetrating earth through Christ's redeeming sacrifice.

The color blue signifies heaven and the color brown earth.

Endorsements

As Emily obeyed God's will and trusted the Lord to lead her, a wonderful story unfolds. From this testimony, the reader's faith will be strengthened and there will be the challenge to trust the Living God completely and move forward with His leading and enabling power.

"Blessed is she who has believed that what the Lord has said to her will be accomplished!"

—Julie Bruce, School Chaplain, Victoria, Australia.

Emily is a woman of faith, filled with the Holy Spirit. I personally have the joy of knowing her since that day in 2001 when we met at All Nations Convocation Jerusalem in Israel. We have kept in touch over the years and I know you will be deeply touched and blessed as I have been as you walk with her as you read her testimony, a journey of love, faith, obedience, divine connections. She walks with God receiving His guidance, provision every area of her life.

—Carole Brown, White Dove Ministries, Tennessee, USA.

The sacrifice, courage and obedience to the voice of the Holy Spirit in Emily's life story reveal God's mission to save and change people's lives even today. You will be deeply touched and blessed as you read her testimony of faith, obedience, divine guidance. My own life and family have forever been changed through Emily's big heart of sacrificial loving kindness.

—Enos Nabudere, Senior pastor,
Eden Life Ministries, Kampala, Uganda.

Emily's testimony shines as a victorious example of faith, courage and love against all odds. Her inspiring story will prepare you to walk in the Lord's will and purposes for your own life. Emily recounts miraculous ways God intervened to cause all things to work for her good because of her constant yielding to the Holy Spirit. I highly recommend this book to provide keys that will guide you to achieve the high prize of your life's calling. "A Journey of Divine Connections" will direct you in the narrow way, the path of the Righteous. Few find it, but Emily did, and is walking it today. Each of us, like Emily, can make a difference in the world and save the lives of many.

—Rev. Rosemary Schindler, Schindler's Ark International.

Readers will be interested to see how God led Emily. Her willingness to follow the Lord is evident. Day to day, year to year faithfulness to the Lord has led her to be a blessing to many people in many places. Her personal journal is bound to stir others to follow Jesus as His true disciple.

—Rev. Jean Darnall, Church on the way,
Van Nuys, California, USA.

A
Journey
of
Divine
Connections

EMILY CHANG

WestBow
PRESS
A DIVISION OF THOMAS NELSON

WestBow Press books may be ordered through booksellers or by contacting:

WestBow Press
A Division of Thomas Nelson
1663 Liberty Drive
Bloomington, IN 47403
www.westbowpress.com
1-(866) 928-1240

Because of the dynamic nature of the Internet, any web addresses or links contained in this book may have changed since publication and may no longer be valid. The views expressed in this work are solely those of the author and do not necessarily reflect the views of the publisher, and the publisher hereby disclaims any responsibility for them.

Any people depicted in stock imagery provided by Thinkstock are models, and such images are being used for illustrative purposes only.

Certain stock imagery © Thinkstock.

ISBN: 978-1-4497-7840-8 (sc)
ISBN: 978-1-4497-7841-5 (hc)
ISBN: 978-1-4497-7839-2 (e)

Library of Congress Control Number: 2012923965

Printed in the United States of America

WestBow Press rev. date: 03/01/2013

Thanks To...

I would like to take this opportunity to express my sincere gratitude to God for His constant faithfulness for His guidance and provision.

I also thank my family and friends for their support and encouragement.

To everyone mentioned in this book and to others whose names have not been included, but who were moved by God to support me with prayer, encouragement, or financial assistance, thank you all so much. May the Lord bless you and keep you, the Lord make His face shine upon you and His peace sustain you continuously!

Foreword

Emily Chang's story is a mosaic of miracles planned and performed by God. The pattern which has emerged is so startlingly bright in its awesome clarity that the amazing grace and mighty miracles of the Living God cannot be denied. The suffering, the sacrifice and the success of Emily are traced in these inspiring pages. God's grace and His hand of selection, protection and direction of her life are abundantly evident throughout her incredible story. All the glory is given gladly to Him.

Emily has witnessed the power of God at work in many countries. She is a woman of great faith and unquestioning obedience to the Lord whom she trusts with all her heart. Because of her obedience to God's commands she has been the channel of many miraculous blessings to desperately needy people.

Emily's world-wide ministry has a unique feature. She is usually moved by the Holy Spirit to cross continents in order to meet one or two particular persons whose deep needs the Lord longs to satisfy. This is a very special part of her ministry reflecting the very personal interest of Jesus in the individual. The Lord who went out of His way to meet the needy woman of Samaria and change her life, still sends His servants across the world to demonstrate His deep personal concern and intense love for individuals. The pages of this book clearly depict this fact.

It has been one of the greatest privileges of my life and ministry to co-operate with Emily in the writing of this exciting book, and it is my prayer that God will glorify His Name, encourage His people and save precious souls as this inspiring story spreads throughout the world!

As you read these pages with faith in your heart, you will be excited to worship and praise the Lord!

Pastor Frank Parker

Preface

For a number of years, many people suggested that I write a book on what I have seen God do in my life, but my answer was always, "No."

However in January 2001, while I was in Uganda to preach and share my testimony at a conference, I was approached by a German publisher and during the course of our conversation, I was asked again, "Why don't you write a book?"

"No, I would prefer not to" was still my answer. At that time I thought that unless God led me to write the book, I would not be able to do it. But he said "Don't hide what God has done in your life."

This was a remark which stirred my mind and I started to seriously pray about it. As a result, God answered affirmatively on several occasions. However, I continued to postpone taking any action on the matter.

While in Los Angeles in February 2007, I met Reverend Jean Darnall, the Youth with a Mission lecturer and a renowned prophetess. Without having ever met me before, Reverend Darnall predicted, "Through your book, your ministry will be enlarged to radio and TV programs." I asked her "What kind of book?" She replied "Your testimony!" even though she had never heard anything about my life. When I received this word, I felt that it was time for obedience. By God's grace, I started writing "A Journey of Divine Connections."

As it will become evident from reading this book, life is full of surprises. In His sovereignty, God is deeply involved with the creation of networks between people and aligning them for His purposes.

Jesus promised that after He ascended into Heaven, He would send the Helper, His Holy Spirit. The same Holy Spirit that demonstrated God's power in the book of Acts continues to work through us today. I know that events in my testimony are the work of the Holy Spirit. These words of Jesus contain this sure promise: But the Helper, the Holy Spirit, whom the Father will send in My name, He will teach you all things, and bring to your remembrance all things that I said to you. (John 14:26)

I pray that readers of this book of testimonies will trust the living God completely and also experience His divine power working in wondrous ways. I give all the glory to God, the Living Master of the Universe.

Emily Chang

FOR YOU, LORD, HAVE MADE ME
GLAD THROUGH YOUR WORK;

I WILL TRIUMPH IN THE WORKS OF YOUR HANDS.

O LORD, HOW GREAT ARE YOUR WORKS!

Psalm 92:4-5

Contents

CHAPTER 1

Preparation for Ministry

God is the Healer—Jehovah Rapha

IN 1957, I WAS BORN in a non-Christian family in South Korea. I had no family support in the Christian faith. I was the only one in the family who went to church despite strong opposition from family members. One of my friends during middle school had told me about Jesus which led me to happily attend church with her every Sunday.

When I was twenty four years old, I married a stainless-steel construction supervisor, employed by POSCO, the largest stainless-steel company in South Korea; the world's third-largest steelmaker today. Prior to my marriage, I had been attending church regularly, but my husband had never even been to one, although not long after our marriage, we began to attend church services together.

One day during the early years of my marriage, my father-in-law visited our home and saw the Bible lying there in full view in the room. He immediately expressed opposition to my Christian faith.

He said, "You are free to do anything you want in your life except go to church!" He was against the Christian way of life because within the Korean culture, it is the usual practice to worship and honor deceased ancestors. My father-in-law knew that as Christians, we would not worship or publicly demonstrate our reverence and worship for our ancestors. He wanted to be greatly venerated by his son, so he opposed Christianity because he thought it would deprive him of this Korean form of respect.

In Korean culture, a daughter-in-law is expected to honor and obey her in-laws. So as a young wife, anxious to please her family, I agreed to my father-in-law's terms, and stopped going to church! The discerning eye can detect that there is a constant spiritual conflict in Korean society arising out of the clash between Confucianism, or idolatry, and the Christian faith.

Four years went by, and then one day a Christian neighbor named Sooni visited in order to tell me about gospel and salvation in Christ. She suggested that I go to church with her. I refused and responded by saying that, although I really wanted to, I couldn't disobey my father-in-law.

Eight days after my neighbor's visit, I was literally struck down with a mysterious affliction. Until that time, I had enjoyed perfect health. Physical pain and suffering were completely new to me.

On that fateful day, my husband left the house for his work as usual, but I could not move and did not have the strength to get out of bed. It was impossible to carry out my daily household routine. When my husband came home that evening, we had to go to a restaurant, as I had been unable to make a meal for us. I cried from the continuous, extreme pain I was suffering the whole time we were there.

We drove to the pharmacist for medication, but nothing relieved the pain. By the time we reached home, I could not even walk the few extra steps to the bedroom to lie down. As I lay on the living room sofa, even the smallest movement brought excruciating pain throughout my entire body.

The next day I went to the hospital for an examination. A thorough diagnosis could not yet be made, however kidney trouble was suspected. As the pain intensified throughout my body, I was soon admitted to a hospital belonging to my husband's company. Intravenous painkillers were administered, which did not reduce the pain at all. It was so intense, even worse than giving birth. I would have been willing to pay all the money I possessed if I could have found relief from the agony, even for one day. That was how desperate I felt.

I remained in hospital for ten days without improvement, and then I was transferred to a bigger hospital in another city where my sister lived. My condition deteriorated, and the flesh on my left calf wasted away to skin and bone, while in my right leg there was no sensation at all. I was not able to pass urine for a few days.

The doctor said I had a very serious condition, and needed to remain in the hospital for at least one year. His advice was very distressing because I was just twenty-eight years old and had two sons, aged two and three. I could not imagine how I could be a good housewife to my husband and mother to my children if I was hospital-bound for a whole year!

While I was in the hospital, the Spirit of God began to convict me that I had neglected the Lord for four years. I realized that God might have had a purpose in allowing this severe illness to afflict me, and I started to ask for forgiveness.

"I'm sorry, Lord!" I sobbed. "I should not have allowed the fear of man to grip me. I know I must fear You, the Lord. I was afraid of my father-in-law, and I felt I had to bow down to his traditions and expectations. From now on, I will only bow down to you, God Most High, Ruler of heaven and earth."

I wept uncontrollably, repenting for having stopped honoring and worshipping God these past four years. After repenting, I gradually felt peace and joy. Fresh boldness and strength were given to me by the Holy Spirit. I felt no longer afraid of man, or of what anyone could do to me. For the first time in my life, I truly feared and honored God above all else.

In God I will praise His word, In God I have put my trust; I will not fear. What can flesh do to me? (Psalm 56:4)

When my husband came to the hospital to see me, I told him that from now on, I could not live and keep on disregarding God. I must come back to the Lord and serve Him totally. He agreed and told me that he also wanted to receive Jesus as Savior and serve God forever. Deuteronomy chapter six verse five states,

"You shall love the Lord your God with all your heart, with all your soul, and with all your might."

God gave us strength and boldness so that we did not fear what others would say any more. My husband and I committed in our hearts that together we would serve the Lord.

"As for me and my house, we will serve the Lord." (Joshua 24:15)

Two weeks after I repented, I began to recover at an incredibly fast rate. This came as a huge surprise to the doctor, who could not explain how I was on my way to complete healing. He exclaimed in amazement, "This can only be a miracle from God!" I was discharged from the hospital after only two weeks, rather than one whole year!

I continued to recover with the help of my sister at her home in Busan. One day, a friend, who knew of my health condition, invited me to a healing conference at a nearby city because she knew that I had not yet fully recovered. After delicate negotiations with my sister, who was not a Christian, I was able to attend with her agreement. This was amazing because my sister did not believe in healing from the Holy Spirit, but trusted only in modern medicine and doctors. She did not believe that prayer for sickness would result in physical healing and make any difference in a person's condition.

While at the healing ministry event, I received an inspired word from the leader of the conference. She said, "Your current situation is a calling from God to return to Him. Your sickness can be completely cured only by prayer, not by modern medication."

At that time, I was still under doctor's orders to take medication. I was also to apply prayer to my situation for total healing from this infirmity. I received prayer and was also told, "You have a gift of healing, and God has allowed you to endure extreme pain. You will now be able to truly sympathize with those who are suffering pain."

Soon after, I felt well enough to leave my sister's and returned to my own home with doctor's instructions to continue to take my first month's prescription of medication. I was expected to continue to take medication for a few months, and my mother had also provided me with a month's worth of expensive Chinese herbal medicine.

However, as soon as I arrived at my home, I asked my Christian neighbour Sooni to bring her pastor to minister to me. Although he had never met me, he had been praying for me while I was in the hospital.

That day, we had a service in my home with my husband and children. I was touched by the Holy Spirit's love and grace. I wept many tears. I was so happy to come back to the Lord.

"Return to Me," says the Lord of Hosts, "and I will return to you." (Zechariah 1:3)

I spoke with the pastor and explained to him her inspired word from the healing conference. I asked, "Is it true that in my case, it is only by prayer that I shall be healed? Can I get rid of all these medicines?" He told me, "It's up to your faith."

I immediately threw all of my costly medication into the rubbish chute! The pastor was amazed by my prompt reaction.

Then I asked him to pray for me that day and the following Sunday morning and evening. After these three prayer times, I was completely healed. My husband and I, when we trusted God, had witnessed a miracle.

Before Jesus died and was resurrected, He promised to send the Holy Spirit to do works that were as great as and even greater than His. That same Spirit is still able to heal and restore people with every kind of illness today. I was proof of His power to do so.

Jesus healed many kinds of sickness, witnessed by Matthew, Mark, Luke, and John.

He healed, the leper, the paralyzed, a woman with a fever, blind men, a mute man, and people who were possessed by unclean spirits. And these are just some examples of the healing miracles that are recorded in the Bible.

"Is anyone among you sick? Let him call for the elders of the church, and let them pray over him, anointing him with oil in the name of the Lord. And the prayer of faith will save the sick, and the Lord will raise him up. And if he has committed sins, he will be forgiven. Confess your trespasses to one another, and pray for one another, that you may be healed. The effective, fervent prayer of a righteous man avails much." (James 5:13-16)

GOD IS JEHOVAH RAPHA—THE HEALER

Born Again

Blessed assurance Jesus is mine!
O what a foretaste of glory divine!
Heir of salvation purchase of God,
Born of His Spirit, washed in His blood.
This is my story this is my song,
Praising my Savior all the day long.
This is my story this is my song,
Praising my Savior, all the day long.
(From the hymn, 'Blessed Assurance,
Jesus is mine. F.J Crosby, 1873)

*A*s a result of God's grace in granting me healing, I became a truly born again Christian. In the past I had attended church, but I had not fully asked Jesus into my heart to be the Lord of my life. My family and I started to put the Lord first in everything we did. We became active members of a church, and my husband, two boys and I were all baptized in water. We did this as a public declaration of our new commitment to give priority to the Holy Spirit's way, rather than the flesh.

For those who live according to the flesh, set their minds on the things of the flesh, but those who live according to the Spirit, the things of the Spirit. For to be carnally minded is death, but to be spiritually minded is life and peace. Because the carnal mind is enmity against God; for it is not subject to the law of God, nor indeed can be. So then, those who are in the flesh cannot please God. But you are not in the flesh, but in the spirit, if indeed the Spirit of God dwells in you. Now if anyone does not have the Spirit of Christ, he is not His. (Romans 8:5-9)

My faith in God grew daily. I loved Him more each day and was overflowing with His love.

One day, my husband and I attended a powerful prayer meeting blessed by the anointing of the Holy Spirit. We were then both baptized in the Holy Spirit and I received the gift of speaking in tongues.

When the day of Pentecost had fully come, they were all with one accord in one place. And suddenly there came a sound from heaven, as of a rushing, mighty wind, and it filled the whole house where they were sitting. Then there appeared to them divided tongues, as of fire, and one sat upon each of them and they were all filled with the Holy Spirit and began to speak with other tongues, as the spirit gave them utterance. (Acts 2:1-4)

After my baptism in the Spirit I was full of fire and passion for God. I told people the truth about the living God who created the universe, yet loves each and every human being. I shared the gospel from scripture about how God has demonstrated His love for us.

For God so loved the world, that He gave His only begotten Son, that whoever believes in Him should not perish but have eternal life. (John 3:16)

I shared with others our need to turn away from sin, to acknowledge Jesus as Lord and Savior and receive forgiveness for our sins. Jesus came as the perfect sacrifice and gave His life for us on the cross. I spoke to many people telling them that faith in Jesus was the only way to eternal life.

Jesus said, "I am the way, the truth and the life. No one comes to the Father, except through me." (John 14:6)

He who has the Son, has life, he who does not have the Son of God, does not have life. (1 John 5:12)

My husband also loved the Lord deeply, and he gave his life and surrendered everything to God. We were overwhelmed by the amazing privilege of becoming children of God. We knew that in Jesus' sacrifice on the cross, and resurrection from the dead, all our sins had been forgiven, and we could look forward to eternity and heaven. There was no longer any fear in death. We had Christ living in us, by His Spirit, and had the hope of a glorious future with no end.

For our citizenship is in heaven, from which we also eagerly wait for the Savior, the Lord Jesus Christ, who will transform our lowly body, that it might be conformed to His glorious body, according to the working by which He is able even to subdue all things to Himself. (Philippians 3:20-21)

We had chosen the narrow path that led to salvation and had no regrets. We knew life in all its fullness quickly grew in faith and developed a firm foundation in Christ that could not be shaken. We became strong believers and our hope in Jesus was rock solid.

Therefore, whoever hears these sayings of mine, and does them, I will liken him to a wise man who built his house on the rock; and the rain descended, the floods came, and the winds blew and beat on that house; and it did not fall, for it was founded on the rock. (Matthew 7:24-25)

"Most assuredly, I say to you, unless one is born of water and the Spirit, he cannot enter the kingdom of God. That which is born of the flesh is flesh, and that which is born of the Spirit is spirit. Do not marvel that I said to you, you must be born again. The wind blows where it wishes, and you hear the sound of it, but cannot tell where it comes from and where it goes, so is everyone who is born of the Spirit." (John 3:3-8)

Our Spirits Shall Sorrow No More

*M*Y FAMILY CONTINUED OUR LIVES in devotion to God and we were full of passion and fire for Him. Every day we would read the Bible, pray together and worship Him. Pleasing the Lord was our number one concern and priority.

In 1988, when I was thirty-one, my two prayer partners and I, went to a Prayer Mountain for fasting and prayer for three days. There are more than five hundred Prayer Mountains in Korea. Prayer Mountain provides a secluded place of prayer for those who desire a place to be alone with God. Our first day there, we spent in fellowship, worship, fasting and prayer.

On the second day, a lady pastor knocked on our room door unexpectedly. When she came in we asked her who she was. She simply replied "God sent me here." We then asked her "How did God send you here?" She said, "The man in charge of this Prayer Mountain telephoned me and asked me to come here to encourage and strengthen three ladies, but I declined because I was too busy and unwilling to travel for two hours. So I hung up. But the Holy Spirit spoke to me saying: 'My three beloved daughters are there, and you must go!' So I immediately obeyed and came."

The lady pastor prayed prophetic prayers with each of us and also encouraged us by sharing her amazing testimony before leaving.

She had experienced harsh opposition from her family for her faith. Before she married she was a committed Christian but then had an arranged marriage with a man whose family held very strong beliefs in Buddhism. This family threw her out of her home after she had tried to share the gospel of Jesus with them. They were extremely offended that she had challenged their beliefs and traditions. Because of this, she had suddenly become homeless with nowhere to go. So she had decided to live at the Prayer Mountain.

During her time there, she cried out to God. She prayed day and night, desperately seeking God in her time of need and salvation for her family. After some time at the Prayer Mountain she had an incredible experience with the Holy Spirit and received power and authority. She also received a prophetic gift and later she became a pastor. Not only this, but her husband and family eventually gave their lives in surrender to God.

After sharing her testimony, she left us but came back again the next day. She laid her eyes on me and spoke directly to me, saying, "I don't even know your name but last night God asked me to pray for you. I prayed for you all night, and I wept much for you."

On that day, she preached to us about earthly death and heaven. The lady pastor asked if my husband and I could do a half-day's fast for forty days. My husband and I followed this advice for forty days and during this period I had three unusual dreams about death.

In the first dream I heard a voice repeat to me three times saying "Hymn number 291." At that time in Korea, the churches used one common hymn book that was identical in title and hymn number.

This particular hymn 291 was usually sung at funerals.

This hymn is titled 'Sweet By And By.' These are some of the lyrics:

There's a land that is fairer than day,
And by faith we can see it afar;
For the Father waits over the way,
To prepare us a dwelling place there.
In the sweet by and by
We shall meet on that beautiful shore.
In the sweet, by and by
We shall meet on that beautiful shore.
(J.P. Webster, 1867)

In the second dream, I was dressed in a traditional white Korean funeral robe, and my neighbors were giving me contributions as is customary at a funeral.

Finally, in the third dream, I saw angels praising God in heaven. These three dreams all related to death and eternity.

At about this time another woman I know whose husband had cancer had been fasting for him for forty days. She also had a vision of two men ascending into heaven dressed in white robes. She could only discern the face of one of the men and it was my husband.

My husband's company provided a private car and a driver as part of his position as construction manager of their new stainless-steel factories. Each morning, the driver would pick my husband up from home to take him to the various building sites to supervise the work at each location. On one particular day, the driver accidentally made a wrong turn, resulting in an express bus slamming into their car, eventually killing them both.

Although the driver died at the accident scene, my husband was taken to hospital where he survived for another fifteen hours then passed away. This explained the dreams and visions preceding this tragedy.

The pain and despair I felt at the loss of my precious husband and father of our two sons could not compare to anything I had ever imagined. I was totally devastated and in shock, not knowing where to turn other than to the Bible. I could only compare my extreme sadness to the Book of Job. Though he was righteous, he also suffered and lost everything, yet he was submissive to the will of God. And Jesus Himself painfully endured the cross for each one of us to receive eternal life and be with Him in Heaven.

This period of my life was very sad and painful; however I could still give thanks to God in the midst of our family's grief. It's easy to be grateful for things that bring us happiness and joy, but God's Word encourages us to give thanks in all circumstances, even in times of affliction and failure and I held fast to this verse from

1Thessalonians 5:18 "in everything give thanks; for this is the will of God in Christ Jesus for you."

I spent time with my children every night, reading the Bible, singing praises, and praying. Our hearts were filled with God's love, which helped us overcome the sudden and tragic sorrow.

As we read the Bible, we discovered in the Bible the histories, prophesies, promises, commands, wisdom, lessons, praises, and the stories of many people of faith. Upon reading those stories, I decided to commit our family to become people of faith. The book of Deuteronomy chapter six verse five says

"You shall love the Lord your God with all your heart, and your soul, and with all your might."

Spiritual Warfare and Persecution at a Family Funeral

*W*HEN MY PASTOR YOUNGTAE LIM heard about what had happened to my husband, he came to the hospital with a coach full of brothers and sisters from our church. They were devastated by the loss of my husband, a wonderful brother in Christ, whom they had so dearly loved, and were eager to comfort me. However, I was to face bitter conflict from my husband's family.

When the time came for my husband to be buried, I was determined to have a Christian rather than a traditional Confucian rooted funeral which was the type my husband's family were wanting. It is the Korean tradition to have a funeral ceremony with a vast array of flowers around a photo of the deceased. Also it is usual to display a large selection of different dishes of food placed on a table in front of the photo. People bow down to the photo out of respect for the person who has passed away. These traditional practices have Confucianism roots which includes the worship of ancestors.

I knew that my husband was fully committed to God before he left us, so any type of funeral other than Christian, was inappropriate.

A spiritual storm exploded around me, and I had to stand up for my faith in Christ and show strength and resilience. I experienced intense persecution from my in-law's family. It was not like anything I had experienced before and I could see that people within my extended family were trying to oppress my witness for Jesus.

I planned to have a Christian way of the funeral service for my husband. My father-in-law realized that I would want to have a Christian funeral service, and was concerned about a family member, a fervent Buddhist. He warned that she would be extremely angry and was worried about ensuing arguments. I told my father-in-law that my husband and I were equally fervent Christians who wanted to do things to honor God and our Savior Jesus Christ. So our Christian funeral service was held in the hospital funeral hall where my husband had breathed his last breath.

Following the service, a family member came into the chamber, verbally attacking me as a Christian. She was enraged and grabbed my cross necklace, ripping it off my body. Next she snatched my Bible, throwing it to the floor a good distance away. She was furious, but I resisted the hostile spirit within her trying to intimidate me.

After this, we went to the burial site. We needed to transport everyone to the cemetery in a funeral coach and it was a four hour journey from the hospital to the gravesite. Again she started to assert her will over mine. She said that no Christians would be allowed in the coach. I was again filled with courage and asked the driver to play a tape of Christian worship music that I had brought with me. I knew that some of the people on the coach would be opposed to this but I wanted to keep the worship of God at the heart of everything that was happening. The driver played the Christian music but as soon as she heard it, she became incensed! She stormed up to the front of the coach and took out my worship tape and put on a Buddhist chanting tape instead. She said to me, "Do you also want to die?"

She said this because she believed that my husband had died as a result of him forsaking the Buddhist way to become a Christian, which of course was not true. She was also very angry and said this to spite me because I had wanted to play Christian worship songs.

However, I remembered these words from the Bible.

I have been crucified with Christ, it is no longer I who live, but Christ lives in me. And the life which I now live in the flesh, I live by faith in the Son of God, who loved me and gave himself for me. (Galatians 2:20)

Earlier on, before we had left the hospital my pastor had told me and my father-in-law that we should drape the coffin with a white robe which had a red cross marked on it, before placing any soil onto the coffin. My in-laws did not want to do this. I told them that it must be done, and we had a long argument.

Eventually one of the in-laws realized that among the many people who had come to the funeral was a Christian lady she knew, so she asked the Christian friend if it was necessary to drape the coffin in the robe as the pastor had suggested. So this Christian lady asked me whether or not my husband had been baptized. I told her that he had, and she then said to my in-laws that my husband's coffin should indeed be draped with the white robe with a red cross on it. After this, they agreed with my decision to drape the coffin with a symbol of my husband's faith in Christ.

Even after this, we continued to have conflicts about other elements of the funeral service. For example, it is another tradition in Korean culture to pour alcohol around the grave. This is done after the coffin has been completely covered over with clods of earth. But, I did not want this practice to be used. To me it had no meaning or significance. I said that I did not want this to happen and a family member became enraged yet again. She was very deceptive and tried to encourage my six year old son to perform the practice instead of me. However, I told my son categorically not to do what she had asked.

King David declared to God, *"into your hands I commit my spirit: You have redeemed me, O Lord God of truth. I have hated those who regard useless idols: But I trust in the Lord." (Psalm 31:5-6)*

I informed everyone there that I would pray around the grave instead of pouring alcohol upon it. This is the prayer that I prayed for everyone to hear.

"Father God, I thank you for my husband's eternal life. Life and death belong to you. You are sovereign and the time of our lives and deaths are in your hands. Thank you Lord that he received you as his personal savior while he was alive and that you said that, *'This is eternal life, that they may know You, the only true God, and Jesus Christ whom You have sent.'* Thank you that he is now with you. Lord, let the people here know that their lives came from you and belong to you."

As soon as I had finished praying, a family member started to scream and shout all kinds of abuse over several hours, using every type of swear word imaginable. The other people at the burial site stood in silence, stunned at this outburst.

At this point, I was again aware of the spiritual conflict. I had God's peace within despite everything that was happening. Even when she was shouting and swearing, I did not react to the situation around me. I had peace and was not hurt, disturbed or even angry. Instead, I prayed for her and was aware that this was really a spiritual battle.

I thought about *Matthew 5:10-12 which says 'Blessed are those who are persecuted for righteousness sake, for theirs is the kingdom of heaven. Blessed are you when they revile and persecute you, and say all kinds of evil against you falsely, for my sake. Rejoice and be exceedingly glad, for great is your reward in heaven, for so they persecuted the prophets who were before you.'*

While I meditated on the scripture, I saw two angels appear above me in a vision. They were there only fleetingly, but this vision comforted me. I had peace and I knew that God was with me and that He knew what had been happening at the funeral service.

You will keep him in perfect peace whose mind is stayed on You, because he trusts in You. Trust in the Lord forever, for in Yahweh the Lord is everlasting strength. (Isaiah 26:3-4)

After hours of verbal abuse, a relative who had observed everything at the service took pity on me. He began to shout at her in order to be heard above her, and he commanded her to stop! He reminded her that I had lost my beloved husband and was suffering an extremely painful and emotional time. He said that of everyone there, my children and I had suffered the greatest loss. He thought it was unbelievable that she would try to add to our suffering and distress by verbally abusing me because of my faith. What I needed was comfort and encouragement. At this point she stopped being abusive.

A week after my husband's burial, all the family returned to the cemetery. I had previously asked the funeral directors for a gravestone engraved with my husband's name with a red cross to be carved into the stone as a reminder that my husband was a Christian. When my in-laws saw the red cross on the gravestone, they erupted with anger and further conflict arose. They told me that they would not allow a red cross to be on his gravestone. They wanted to destroy it, and put up a stone that had a Buddhist symbol engraved on it as opposed to the cross.

I refused their requests so each one came to me to try to make me back down from my decision. They tried rebuking, cajoling, and persuading me, but time after time I refused and would not consider their plans. From morning to afternoon this went on, but no one could dissuade me from my original choice and conviction that a cross should be on my husband's memorial stone. They thought that I was just being stubborn in nature; however, for me there was no debate or negotiation. I was acutely aware that I was fighting a spiritual battle, and that I must achieve the victory of proclaiming Christ, even in this situation. I held onto the truths of this scripture which applied to the conflict that was going on around me:

For we do not wrestle against flesh and blood, but against principalities, against powers, against the rulers of the darkness of this age, against spiritual hosts of wickedness in the heavenly places. (Ephesians 6:12)

Eventually, everyone became tired of trying to change my decision because I would not entertain the thought of a Buddhist themed gravestone for my husband, a strong Christian. It would have been completely nonsensical and would have dishonored the fact that he had died in Christ and was in heaven as a result.

So myself and most of those present at the funeral went down to the restaurant that was situated at the foot of the graveyard. Whilst everyone else was eating I was meditating on Jesus and praying continually to God asking Him to protect the gravestone with the red cross.

Everyone had come down to the restaurant except my father-in-law, a family member and my eldest son. They were still further up the mountain near the burial site. My father-in-law was talking with my eldest son. He told my son that he and his relatives could not stand to see the red cross on the memorial stone and he asked my son, "What can we do about this?"

He was exasperated and sighing when asked this, and didn't expect an answer from his six year old grandson. However, my son replied "Without the red cross, my dad cannot be in heaven." This was my six year old son's faith and best explanation of the nature of salvation: that Jesus's death on the cross and the shedding of His blood for our sins, made a way for us to be forgiven and go to heaven.

"I am the way, the truth, and the life. No-one comes to the Father except through me." (John 14:6)

My father-in-law broke down in tears because of the power of my son's words given to him by the Holy Spirit. My father-in-law then said to him, "Very well, we will allow the grave stone with red cross to remain."

My son's words had broken the resistance and hostility in my father-in-law's heart to the cross of Christ and from then on, the dispute between my in-laws and myself ended. The spiritual conflict that surrounded me was finished and our family had won the victory for Christ.

This testimony clearly demonstrates that the Lord gave me the victory in every conflict which He allowed to come my way.

I have set the Lord always before me: Because He is at my right hand I shall not be moved. (Psalm 16:8)

The Lord is my light and my salvation: Whom shall I fear? The Lord is the Strength of my life: of whom shall I be afraid? (Psalm 27:1)

JEHOVAH NISSI—THE LORD MY BANNER OF VICTORY

God's Calling and My Destiny

*I*T WAS VERY DISTRESSING TO lose my dear husband so suddenly and I started to wonder about the lady pastor from the Prayer Mountain who had wept and prayed for me that whole night. I desperately wanted to know about any message that she had received from the Lord at that night, but I didn't have a way to contact her. So I prayed to God and asked that He would somehow connect us. The Lord answered my prayer in a wonderful way.

It was not long after that the two of us met unexpectedly at the bus terminal, although we lived in completely different areas. In amazement, I grabbed her hand and said, "I prayed to God and asked Him to make it possible for me to meet you."

Her first response was, "I heard the news that a person from your husband's company was in an accident. Was it your husband?" I replied "Yes, did you know this would happen?"

She answered, "I knew."

I asked her to come to my house and reveal to me what the Lord had shown her that night after our first meeting at the Prayer Mountain. She came immediately and described her vision of my husband going to heaven. She also was given a further revelation that God would use me greatly throughout the nations!

This was something that I could never have imagined! I had been happy in my role as a mother and a wife, and enjoyed having a sphere of influence for God in my home. Now God was going to use me to influence all nations for His glory? This was a complete turn in my life's direction. It made me remember the time when Jesus called Peter and Andrew. These men were just simple fishermen, just as I felt myself to be an ordinary woman, and Jesus called them to follow Him, and become fishers of men, making disciples wherever they went.

The Bible states in Matthew 4:18-22: *And Jesus walking by the Sea of Galilee, saw two brothers, Simon called Peter and Andrew his brother, casting a net into the sea for they were fishermen. Then He said to them, "Follow me, and I will make you fishers of men." They immediately left their nets and followed him. And then going on from there he saw other brothers, James the son of Zebedee, and John his brother, in the boat with Zebedee their father, mending their nets. He called them and immediately they left the boat and their father and followed Him.*

It was so wonderful that God had shown me His calling for my life. It gave me hope and helped me to have the courage to look towards the future with a sense of anticipation. I was able to focus on the good that was to come, rather than dwell only on the past. Also, I had complete assurance that my husband was alive with Jesus in heaven and this I knew without any shadow of doubt.

I could not stop thinking about God's loving kindness and grace. In such a timely way He had rescued me from being overcome by grief and depression. This is one of the amazing things about my God: He is able to bring beauty for ashes in people's lives. Death is an inevitable outcome for all human beings, and the untimely nature of my husband's death made it all the more upsetting. However, God is the Lord of every circumstance and was giving me the opportunity and honor of doing His will despite my tragic loss.

For in the Christian life there is always a blessing in every storm because the scripture states:

All things work together for good to those who love God, to those who are called according to His purpose. (Romans 8:28)

I completely surrendered everything to God and offered myself as an empty vessel, praying that He would always be with me and would lead me in the right direction.

This is described in the Shepherd's Psalm: *The Lord is my*

shepherd: I shall not want. He makes me to lie down in green pastures; He leads me beside the still waters. He restores my soul; He leads me in the paths of righteousness for His name's sake. (Psalm 23:1-3)

This was my heart towards God: *I will love you, O Lord, my strength, fortress and my deliverer, my stronghold. I will call upon the Lord, who is worthy to be praised. (Psalm 18:1-3)*

JEHOVAH SHALOM—THE LORD MY PEACE

CHAPTER 2

Building Bridges

God's Preparation for a New Direction

ECAUSE OF ALL THIS SUFFERING and loss, I had a greater sense of the fleeting nature of life. God gave me a new level of boldness to share the gospel with friends who came to visit and comfort me. I was acutely aware of the fact that these people all needed salvation in Christ and that any of them could pass away unexpectedly at any time. People who visited me were surprised when I witnessed to them and told them about Jesus in that situation. They were expecting that I would be utterly crushed by grief and sadness.

However, I had strength in the Lord and my passion for Him remained the same in every type of circumstance. I had to stand firm for God in my situation. I could either wallow in grief, sadness and depression over the loss I had suffered, or I could stand strong in my faith, give thanks despite my circumstances and share with my children the wonderful promise of glory for those who are in Christ. I had to consider what would be the wisest way to cope for the sake of myself and my children. I wanted to honor God and also encourage them to love God and honor Him in all circumstances. Encouraging them and surrounding them with love was my priority.

Every day we read the Bible together and we sang songs of worship that focused on our citizenship in heaven and the hope we had in God. Because of this, my children were able to cope with the circumstances they faced and were not overcome with sadness. As a family, we had unfailing hope in God and the Holy Spirit sustained us all.

Commit your way to the Lord, trust also in Him, and He will bring it to pass. He shall bring forth your righteousness as the light, and your justice as the noonday. (Psalm 37:5-6)

God gave me beautiful dreams about heaven every night over a period of two months. This comforted me and reassured me and helped me not to be overwhelmed by my situation.

Therefore, having been justified by faith, we have peace with God through our Lord Jesus Christ, through whom also we have access by faith into this grace in which we stand, and rejoice in the hope of the glory of God. And not only that, but we also have glory in tribulations, knowing that tribulation produces perseverance: and perseverance, character; and character, hope. Now hope does not disappoint, because the love of God has been poured out in our hearts by the Holy Spirit who was given to us. (Romans 5:1-5)

God had wonderfully shown me His Sovereignty. I knew that

I had a calling from God to bless the nations and be instrumental in the work of God in various ways around the world.

Psalm 32:8 states: *I will instruct you and teach you in the way you should go: I will guide you with My eye.*

So in obedience to his leading I began a two year missionary training course in Korea.

One year passed, and in the summer of 1989, representatives of Operation Mobilization, (O.M) a mission organization, carried out recruitment for a short term mission called "Love Europe." I felt God's calling to join the mission, and therefore travelled to the conference in Offenburg, Germany.

There were seven thousand delegates from over seventy nations in attendance. We were split into smaller teams depending on our choice of location for mission. For example, I was in a group that would be going on a mission to London.

In my group, I struggled to understand the lead speaker. He was speaking English very quickly with a Scottish accent and I was inexperienced in my understanding of spoken English. Therefore, I was extremely grateful when Max, a young student from Edinburgh University in Scotland, sat down next to me and, realising my difficulty, simplified the message so that I was able to understand the speaker. Max was twenty years old, and it transpired that our meeting was, again, not by chance. God had planned it ahead of time.

Max had prayed earlier in the year concerning his use of time during the summer vacation, and had been led to attend the "Love Europe." conference. He had a mentor, Paul who was a Christian minister with a prophetic gift.

From a prophetic message, Paul told Max that God had a special reason for him to attend this conference. He, Max, would be meeting a particular person who was to play an important role in God's future purposes. Over the course of the Love Europe event, Max sensed that I was the one.

When Max returned to Edinburgh, he met with Paul and explained about his meeting with a lady named Emily Chang from Korea. They prayed together and the Lord confirmed that I was indeed the person that Max was meant to meet.

During their prayer, God spoke to Paul and said, "Intercede for Emily and her family to fulfil My plan for her ministry." All of this was unknown to me until sometime later.

I really appreciated all the assistance Max had given me at the Love Europe conference and during the mission to London. He had helped me to overcome the language barrier which was invaluable. Because of my gratitude to Max, I kept in touch with him after I returned to Korea, writing letters, calling him, and sending gifts. He kindly invited me to his parents' home in Glasgow for Christmas, but sadly I was unable to make another long distance trip within the same year.

Six months later, I had another opportunity to go to Germany. Initially, I had planned to stay two weeks for a mission but all my work was completed in ten days. I remembered Max's previous invitation and so I thought I could use the four days to visit him in Scotland as I was already in Europe. I telephoned Max and asked whether I could visit him for four days.

He replied "I knew you were coming!" I was very taken aback and surprised by this and asked him how he knew this.

"God told us you are coming and that we should wait and prepare for your visit. We are waiting." he replied.

Max and his mentor, Paul, had been interceding for me every day. I realized that this was the guidance of the Holy Spirit and knew it was the right time to visit. I was warmly welcomed when I came to Scotland by Paul, his wife and their many children and Max.

I enjoyed fellowship with other believers for two days in Edinburgh where I spoke to a group of Christians in a church hall. Paul interviewed me about Korea and the Korean church and I shared some of my testimony.

I visited Glasgow where I was invited by Max to meet with his friends and spent time with people from his mother's church. We shared times of fellowship and personal testimony. I also told them of some of the amazing things that God was doing within the Korean church.

I thought this would be my first and last visit to Scotland and could not imagine returning again. It was a short visit, but was enriched with the fellowship of friends who met me; I am sure, through God's arrangement. I experienced Scotland's wild winter weather, had a taste of Scottish culture and understood more about the country.

During my eventful journey back home from Germany to Korea, God performed an amazing act of intervention.

I had to make my round-trip journey back to Korea from Germany's Frankfurt International Airport. I took the train to Stuttgart where I would get a flight to Frankfurt but after boarding the train, I realized that I had lost my train ticket when the ticket inspector came to check it. I was confused because I couldn't find it anywhere, when in fact I knew that I had indeed bought one. The inspector believed my explanation and let me stay on the train without paying for another ticket.

Later, on a further stretch of the train journey to Stuttgart, another female inspector came to check our tickets. She did not speak any English so she could not understand what I was saying about what had happened to my ticket. She went through to another carriage of the train and brought back a Swiss man who spoke both English and German. I told him what had happened. He trusted me and believed my explanation and translated it to the ticket inspector. She was also sympathetic and allowed me to remain on the train without buying another ticket.

The Swiss man asked me if I had any money with me and I told him that I did not and I did not need it. I had the flight tickets for my journey already purchased and I had already used all the cash I had brought with me. He offered me money and insisted that I have it for emergencies just in case. At first I refused, but he would not take no for an answer. We kept disagreeing about this and I kept insisting that I did not need any money. Eventually, I received his generous gift of around sixty dollars. It transpired that he was also a Christian, so for a while we sat together on the train and talked about God.

When I eventually arrived in Stuttgart, I found that the domestic flight to Frankfurt had been cancelled! So I was very concerned, as I would miss the most important flight from Frankfurt back to Korea.

I spoke to a staff member at Stuttgart airport and explained my situation and as she could not help, I asked her to telephone the Korean airline instead. The Korean air staff member told me that the next flight from Frankfurt to Korea would be in another seven days' time and she advised me to go to Paris on an overnight train, and then onto Korea the following day. For this, I needed to purchase a train ticket.

I could never have planned for this unexpected turn of events and it was by the grace of God that I had the exact funds to travel. This was only as a result of the Swiss Christian man's insistence that I take the money he was offering although I didn't believe I would need it. God had miraculously arranged this divine appointment and had made provision for this situation which He knew would arise.

Even though I had lost my train ticket, it had been a blessing from God for it had led to me meeting the man who would give me funds for an even worse emergency later on in my journey home.

And we know that all things work together for good to those who love God, to those who are called according to His purpose. (Romans 8:28)

Prophet with the Message "Move to Scotland"

Paul and Max in Korea

S EVEN MONTHS LATER, IN SEPTEMBER 1990, Max and Paul came to visit me in Korea. Many things were on Max's heart that he wanted to achieve during his time in my country. He prayed for specific opportunities in certain areas. For example, he hoped to teach the Bible and English and to share the gospel with young people. He was keen to learn New Testament Greek and visit China and Japan.

Amazingly, God made it possible for Max to do all the things he had hoped for during the six months he was based in Korea. He used me to help connect Max to all of the right people who would help him fulfil the desires of his heart.

Max totally trusted God to meet his financial needs and provision was always there at the right time. This even included trips to China and Japan.

Moreover, a pastor friend of mine, an expert in the Greek language was able to give Max lessons providing him with a fantastic foundation in the language. Even this unusual prayer request was met by God in an amazing way.

Max, Paul and I visited the most well-known Prayer Mountain and attended several churches where Paul preached and shared his testimony. We all had a very blessed time and enjoyed being led by God.

Time passed quickly, and on the last night before Paul was due to leaves for Scotland, two pastors and their wives came to my home to wish him farewell. On that night, while we were talking and sharing, there was a mighty visitation of the Holy Spirit. We prayed, prophesied, spoke in tongues, received interpretations and spent time with God from nine at night until five the next morning! I felt that it was like the experience of the people in the upper room when they first received the Holy Spirit.

Now when the Day of Pentecost had fully come, they were all with one accord in one place. And suddenly there came a sound from heaven, as of a rushing mighty wind, and it filled the whole house where they were sitting. Then there appeared to them divided tongues, as of fire, and one sat upon each of them. And they were filled with the Holy Spirit and began to speak with other tongues, as the Spirit gave them utterance. (Acts 2:1- 4)

Paul was due to leave at six in the morning for the airport but because of the visitation of the Holy Spirit, none of us had had a chance to sleep! Both pastors and their wives had left by then but Paul remained with me. We had one hour remaining when Paul turned to me and said something which, after all the rejoicing, sent a chill into my heart.

"Emily, I will now tell you the reason why I came to Korea. God has given me a message to deliver to you. He is telling you to move to Scotland, just you, not with your children."

I felt weak and my mind went numb. My immediate response was, "Impossible!"

The prospect of me moving without my boys distressed me greatly.

My two sons at that time were only six and eight years old. I could not imagine them growing up without a mother, especially as their father had passed away. I also knew that people would perceive me, as a missionary to Scotland who abandoned her children and avoided her responsibilities. I was fearful of the persecution which would certainly follow if I proposed this course of action. All these thoughts came crowding into my mind as I faced Paul. How could he even think that this was God's instruction for me! I voiced my objections to Paul and he said, "I know, I know. When I heard this from God in Scotland, I struggled with the content of this message and I told Him that I would not be able to say this to you. I pleaded with God to give another message for you, but He told me only, "Go and tell her!" So I had to obey Him and that is why I came here. For three weeks I have watched you and your children and have seen the special bond between you all and it has been even more difficult to say this than I expected."

Paul was almost in tears and I realized how painful it had been for him to give me this message.

I was astounded by this sudden and unexpected message.

For some months I was in a conflict about this matter. I could not imagine leaving my children to go to Scotland and had never even considered the possibility of living there! The idea of being separated from my children was so painful, especially after all that we had already been through as a family. I tried to ignore this distressing message, or to deny that somehow I had even heard it. However, I had to trust that Paul's message was from God Himself, especially when I recalled the night in my home, when there had been a mighty visitation of the Holy Spirit and we had all prayed together. Thus, I considered very seriously this direction from God.

Eventually, after struggling for some time on my own with these thoughts and questions, I informed my children about the message from the Lord. I couldn't believe it when they responded, "Obey God, otherwise you will end up in the whale's stomach like Jonah in the Bible!"

I was amazed at their faith and, considering that they were so young, their firm understanding of what it means to trust and obey God and the consequences which may arise when we do not obey. They seemed to have faith beyond their years.

On hearing these words I saw them to sleep. My precious, precious children! I cried out to the Lord all night long, sobbing uncontrollably and pleading for my children. I begged Him to make another way, a way in which I could obey him, but also keep us together as a family. I repeated to God what the children had said to me saying, "They didn't care about their lives but they asked me to obey You." It was the most agonizing experience.

Even though it was very difficult and painful, I decided that there was no option but to obey the Lord. I felt helpless, not knowing anything about how I would survive alone in a foreign country like Scotland. I would be totally dependent upon God in every way.

One night I had a dream in which a lady from the church below my apartment came to ask me if I could move out by March 4th. At first, when I woke up, I did not understand the meaning of the dream. However, the day after this experience, the pastor from the church below my home came to visit. He wanted to enquire about a practical matter which would affect me. The church was looking to accommodate mission training students within the same building as the church. He was wondering if it might be possible for me to consider moving to another place, so that his church could use my apartment to house these students starting from the fourth of March! This made sense of the dream of the previous night. It seemed that God had been preparing me to move, so immediately I agreed to relocate to free up the space for his mission training ministry.

Later that day, I shared with a friend from my church, Eunsook, about the difficult decision I had to make. After hearing about my internal struggle she immediately said, "You obey God and I will care for your children. If you obey God, your life and that of your children will be richly blessed. If you don't obey God, you and your children's lives will lack God's blessing."

I discovered that Eunsook had a good reason for offering her services. When she was fifteen years old, her father, a pastor, had died unexpectedly. Her mother had been left to care for Eunsook and her four siblings. Later, her mother had been called by God to do mission work and God had sent several American missionaries to initiate the process. However, she believed her priority in life was that of provider for her children. She wanted to be self-reliant and earn money through her own ability. Eunsook's mother did not realize that if she trusted God, He would then be the one to provide for her and meet all of her family's needs. Nevertheless, she decided that she was unable to take this step of faith and trust, and lost this opportunity for service.

Eunsook believed that, as the result of this decision, the life of the family had been one of continuous struggle and had really lacked God's blessing. This was why Eunsook encouraged me so strongly to follow God's leading and obey Him.

After her offer to care for my children, Eunsook discovered that a person was interested in buying her house. She was amazed as she had been trying to sell the house for two years. She had been earnestly seeking God in daily prayer and was desperate for Him to intervene. On the day that she offered to look after my children, she sold the house for her asking price! The family who bought it wanted to move in by March 4th! This was God's perfect timing at work because her house had insufficient room for my children. On that night for the first time, she heard God's loving voice say, "Eunsook, I will bless you." All her family were pleased to have my children and believed that supporting them would be an amazing source of blessing from God.

The fact that the family wanted to move into Eunsook's house on March 4th was further confirmation for me that I was doing the right thing in obedience to God. Their request to move in on that date matched the request from the pastor of the church as well. It was God's perfect timing.

That day, I went with Eunsook to the estate agent and found a big four bedroom house that would be suitable for her family and my children. I immediately put down a deposit to reserve the house and reasoned that my children would now have enough room.

On the same night, I visited my in-laws and other relatives and announced to them that I would be going to Scotland by myself and that my friend would be looking after my children. They were absolutely furious and could not understand how I could go to a foreign country without my children. They were shocked and outraged and could not believe the decision I had made. They threatened to set fire to Eunsook's house just because she had encouraged me to go alone to Scotland!

Although they were not serious in their threats, their statements revealed the intensity of their anger. They tried to persuade me not to do this, but I kept repeating emphatically that I had to go and that I had made my final decision. Again my extended family were persecuting me for the decision I had made to obey and glorify God.

In his outrage at my decision, my father-in-law gave me an

ultimatum and said I had three options to consider, and three days in which to reach a decision.

He said that, Number one; if I were to leave for Scotland without my children, he would break the in-law relationship, bring the children from my friend's house, and never let me see my children again.

Number two; I could go to Scotland, but only if I took my children.

Number three; I could live in Korea with my children as a normal family. .

My only possible answer was the first option because that would allow me to obey God's specific command. This would mean that I would be unable to see my children any more. If I chose either of the other two options it would mean blatantly disobeying God. I knew I must tell my relatives that I would choose the first option so I fasted for three days, seeking God and praying.

I also sang the hymn 'There's a royal banner' with these lyrics:

There's a royal banner given for display
to the soldiers of the king
As an ensign fair we lift it up today,
while as ransomed ones we sing
Marching on, marching on
For Christ count everything but loss,
And to crown Him king, toil and sing
'Neath the banner of the cross.
(D.W. Whittle, 1887)

And 'Go forward'

Go forward Saints, towards the gate of heaven,
Let woes and hindrances never you dismay.

Led by the Spirit by the Father given
How can you faint and why this delay?
Forward still, forward still!
Storming the heights for heaven's gate,
Eyes firm fixed on Zion and victory!
At the portals wait you unnumbered angels,
Eager to share heaven's ecstasy.
(R. Lowry)

I promised God that I would choose what He wanted although it would come with a price and much persecution. I asked God to soften my father-in-law's heart.

When I returned after three days of fasting, the Lord had answered my prayer in an incredible way! My father-in-law asked me for my answer to his ultimatum and I bravely told him that I had chosen the first option.

To my surprise, he acknowledged my answer and told me that my friend was a very kind person to offer to look after my children! He agreed to visit my children once in a while. He allowed me to leave for Scotland, alone in peace. After only three days his entire attitude had changed and God had done an amazing work in softening his heart.

After this agreement, my children and I moved to the new house with my friend's family. Then I bought just one ticket for myself to travel to Scotland. I telephoned Paul to tell him of my journey details. In the meantime God had spoken to him about me. After I acquainted him with my travel arrangements, the first thing he said was, "Bring the boys."

I could not believe what I was hearing! I asked him over and over the same question, "WHAT?" After all of the turmoil I had been through in coming to a decision to leave Korea without my young children and the persecution, I had encountered from my family and friends around me I was astounded to hear that I indeed should bring my children with me! What Paul was telling me was not sinking in and it did not make sense to me at all!

Paul then said, "God said that He tested your faith as He tested Abraham and you passed." Simultaneously he added, "God acknowledges your faith as Abraham's faith and He will bless your family and has said that you are to bring your children with you."

I was flabbergasted! I had literally moved house, made arrangements for the care of my children, dealt with confrontations with my relatives, and all of this had been a test! I was almost speechless. It took some time for all of this to sink in.

When eventually I grasped the reality of what had happened, I was thrilled and happy that I had passed God's test. I had passed my test of faith because my priority in life was to put God first in every way.

Now the LORD had said to Abraham: "Get out of your country, from your kindred and from your father's house, to a land that I will show you. (Genesis 12:1)

Now it came to pass after these things that God tested Abraham, and said to him, "Abraham!" And he said, "Here I am." And He said, "Take now your son, your only son Isaac, whom you love, and go to the land of Moriah, and offer him there as a burnt offering on one of the mountains of which I shall tell you." So Abraham rose early in the morning and saddled his donkey, and took of his young men with him, and Isaac his son; and he split the wood for the burnt offering, and arose and went to the place of which God had told him. (Genesis 22:1-3)

And Abraham stretched out his hand and took the knife to slay his son. But the Angel of the LORD called to him from heaven and said, "Abraham, Abraham!" And he said, "Here I am." And He said. "Do not lay your hand on the lad, or do anything to him;

for now I know that you fear God, seeing you have not withheld your son, your only son, from Me." (Genesis 22:10-12)

At first, even my boys were surprised at this change in our plans but eventually we were all overjoyed that we could be together. They had been willing to let me move away, and had even encouraged me to obey God. They were obviously very happy that God was allowing us to relocate as a family. I praise God who not only saw my faith but also the faith of my children.

On the other hand, my friend Eunsook was not overjoyed as she believed that caring for my children would continue to bring blessing to her and her family. But God sees people's hearts and had seen her willingness to support us. Whether she looked after my children in the long-term or not, God's love for her remained the same.

Although God had said that I could take my children when I moved, Eunsook suggested that I first go to Scotland for a short period to seek God's will for our future life there. I decided to do this and she agreed to look after my boys whilst I was away for that time.

In May 1991, I came to Edinburgh by myself for two months. I stayed with Paul's family for the first three weeks and then God connected me with people who were able to help in several practical ways. He also orchestrated contacts with people who could make arrangements for me to have a quiet accommodation while I sought God's will. I came to Scotland as an adventure of faith and God proved Himself to be completely faithful and dependable yet again.

Before I left Korea, a pastor mentioned that his cousin was studying for his doctorate in computer science at Edinburgh University. I asked him for contact information of this man but his cousin's address or telephone number was unknown to him. The only thing he was able to tell me was his cousin's name which was Yong Lee.

So I wrote to the University with a very general address on it which said 'Yong Lee, Computer Science Department, Edinburgh University.' In the letter I introduced myself and provided Paul's phone number so that he could contact me. Soon I received a call from Yong with his address and telephone number. He kindly invited me to his home so I visited him. I was so grateful to meet another Korean living in Edinburgh. He happened to be the Chairman of the Korean Society, and gave me useful information on how to live as a foreigner in Scotland. He also knew of a perfect place for me to stay where I could seek God in prayer.

This led me to spend five weeks in a private room where I prayed and fasted for one week. During this time, I asked God many questions, as I still had so much I wanted to know about my move to this new country. I sought God on many issues and asked for reasons why God had called me to be in Scotland. He told me that I was here to intercede for revival in Scotland, that Scotland would be my base, and that He would send me to many nations from here.

During this time, I began to understand more about Scotland. It seemed strange that God would ask me to intercede for a country which is already considered to be a Christian nation. Yet I quickly learned that, even with a rich Christian heritage, there may only be few truly committed believers. From my research I discovered that historically, the Scots had once a powerful and devout Christian community, sending out many missionaries into the world. The background for this action came from 1900 years ago when Scotland was outside the Roman Empire and was attracting early church believers. They had journeyed here with the gospel, seeking freedom from the Roman Empire.

The preaching and the miracles that followed converted this northern region, establishing Christian centers that resisted the influence of idolatry throughout the Imperial Church of Constantine's reign.

In keeping with this strong Christian heritage, Andrew, a disciple of Jesus, is Scotland's patron Saint. He was the first to declare among the Galileans that he had found the Messiah and was later martyred on a cross. It is this emblem that is represented on Scotland's national flag.

But now, it was Scotland needing the missionaries from other countries to revive her Christian faith and to build the kingdom of God once again. It seemed clear that God wanted me to participate in this re-establishment of His Church.

However, even though learning about this new country was important, more immediate practical matters had to be addressed such as where I should live, which school my children should attend, and how I should start to intercede in obedience to my calling. Faithfully, God answered and provided everything.

During my visit, Yong encouraged me to attend a weekend gathering of Koreans from different cities of Scotland and there I made connections with people who could help me later when I moved permanently. This was a great blessing from God. He had worked in wonderful ways in answer to the prayers of my heart during my week of fasting.

During my seclusion in the private room, I sought God's plan for His future accommodation for my family. I asked God to clearly show me His miraculous provision.

On the last day of fasting, I received a telephone call from a Korean student named Ha, asking whether I needed accommodation. I immediately thought this was the answer for which I was waiting. Ha informed me that Yong, the computer science student, had made a sudden decision to move to Australia.

Ha suggested that I should consider moving into Yong's

apartment. However, I felt it was unsuitable for me because there was only one bedroom and the kitchen was very tiny. Only one person could fit into it at a time! Because I love to cook for others, I really felt that this area of my ministry would be inhibited by the tiny kitchen. I disliked it intensely, but was still willing to consider it. If God had chosen it for me, then I would submit to His will. I wanted to know more about this offer, so I asked, "Why do you recommend this particular apartment for me?"

Ha explained "I am going to do further research in Lebanon for six months and I urgently need someone to store my belongings while I am away. I do not have very much, so would it be possible to pack my belongings into the corner of the living room? The monthly rent for the apartment is three hundred pounds, but I will pay you one hundred pounds per month for six months to store my belongings."

It felt like God had brought this situation to my attention so that I could help Ha. God teaches us to love our neighbors as ourselves and that it is more blessed to give than receive. I knew it would be selfish of me to reject the apartment because I didn't like it, if God wanted me to be selfless and offer my help. I had to trust and obey Him.

The Holy Spirit prompted me to say to Ha, "You can move your things into the apartment, and I will look after your belongings. You don't need to pay me for that. But the problem is that I won't need the apartment for two months because I am going to Korea and will come back with my children after that. However, because you urgently require a place to put your belongings, I will take the apartment."

So I accepted God's choice for me by faith and because I believed that someone else's needs were being met as well.

Ha paid for the two months' rent of six hundred pounds while the apartment was unoccupied as I was back in Korea. It was perfectly arranged so that my boys and I could move straight in when we arrived in Scotland. Yong left me all his furniture and household appliances so that I did not have to purchase new ones. He also sold me his car for a reasonable price.

Jehovah Jireh was at work! When we trust and obey God, He provides for us and takes care of us. He is even interested in the things that might seem too small or insignificant to others. He shows such love to us.

I returned to Korea and shared various testimonies of God's provision during the two months that I had sought Him. Those who had doubted my decision and had previously persecuted me now thought of me as woman of great faith. They could see that the Lord had done amazing things!

Without faith it is impossible to please Him, for he who comes to God must believe that He is, and that He is a rewarder of those who diligently seek Him. (Hebrew 11:6)

To obey is better than sacrifice. (1 Samuel 15:22)

JEHOVAH ROHI—THE LORD MY SHEPHERD

The Fruits of Obedience

*G*OD REVEALED HIMSELF TO ABRAHAM as Jehovah Jireh, the Lord will provide. He is the same God who provided for all my needs originating from my move to Scotland from Korea.

My children and I left everything we knew and loved in our homeland, and moved to Scotland, a country God had called us to. My sons aged seven and nine and I had to adapt to a new culture and way of life. I thought of the words of Jesus in

Mark 10:29-30: "Truly I say to you, there is no one who has left house or brothers or sisters or mother or father or children or farms for My sake and for the gospel's sake, but that he shall receive a hundred times as much now in the present age, houses and brothers and sisters and mothers and children and farms, along with persecutions; and in the age to come, eternal life."

In September 1991, we arrived with great peace in our hearts, for God had provided a home for us in a fantastic way. We moved into the apartment, the one which had initially been dismissed as unsuitable by me, in acceptance that it was the one that God had provided. We all trusted that our future there was held by Him. I submitted to God's will and received His provision with thankfulness. God planned to bless us wonderfully in this new home.

My children commenced their education in Bruntsfield Primary School, which was famous for being the former school of the Hollywood film star, Sean Connery. We were pleased that it was a school with an excellent reputation. My sons had made a tremendous sacrifice in coming to a new country. I was very concerned that they settle in to their new classes quickly.

On the day they started school, I gave each of their class-mates special Korean pencils and erasers as gift. They were decorated with popular cartoon characters and inscribed with a Bible verse in Korean, "Give thanks in all circumstances." The children were delighted with their gifts, and it created a warm and welcoming atmosphere for my sons on their first day. Despite some language difficulties, they were soon befriended by the other pupils, became instantly popular and more importantly, were very happy. We have fond memories of that period in our lives.

Because they felt accepted by the pupils and teachers, my boys were confident enough to excel in their school work. They made several friends, one of whom was an Australian boy named Hamish who had come with his family for an extended stay in Scotland. He often came to our home and was soon joined by his brother Andrew.

The boys spent many hours in each other's company and cultivated a strong friendship. Andrew and Hamish came to our home after school because their mother worked late as a teacher in a town just outside Edinburgh. The boys enjoyed playing together and eventually I began to form a bond with their lovely Christian mother, Julie. She had been praying for many months asking God for sending her a good Christian friend and we had great times of sharing and talking about God's love while our children played together.

Our friendship developed in a wonderful way but sadly, six months after we had known each other Julie and her family had to return to their home country, Australia, and she hoped that I and my boys would consider coming too. However, I knew that God had directed me to Scotland.

Before they left for home, the family sold their car to me quite cheaply for a birthday present. This was a tremendous blessing for I had given my previous car to Paul, whose large family desperately needed it. Over the years, Julie and I have continued to maintain a very precious friendship and have kept in touch with each other.

Looking back, I see the wise provision of God in the apartment where I first lived with my children in Edinburgh. It was due to the location of my home that my boys went to an excellent school where I made many friends and met other Christian parents. God arranged everything and it was wonderful to receive the blessing of forming strong friendships with other people who loved the Lord.

With great joy I was able to extend hospitality to these friends in our home. They were always eager to taste and eat the delicious Korean food which was cooked in my tiny kitchen. Every Wednesday I invited them for a prayer meeting which soon became very multi-cultural. About fifteen people of various nationalities attended and we would rejoice greatly with singing, praising, and praying in a variety of languages and styles and worshiping God accompanied by music on the piano.

I wondered whether my neighbor in the apartment below would be bothered by the noise. I visited to a gentleman in his seventies who occupied the apartment below. He was very understanding and said that we could continue with our activities because he was deaf in one ear. His ninety four years old mother was also totally deaf! God had chosen a place where even my neighbor would not be disturbed by our praises and prayers! I was amazed at how God was at work.

This neighbor was such a blessing as I would, on occasions, accidentally lock myself out of my apartment. He would then get his ladder, climb up to and through my window and open the door to let me in! He was always so patient and gracious. I felt like God had meant for me to live above him.

One night while I was asleep, my washing machine water pipes burst, leaking water onto the floor. It soaked down into my neighbor's kitchen ceiling, causing it to collapse. I was so sorry, and felt very badly about the situation, especially because he was always so good to us. He asked me whether my apartment was insured. It was not, and I was very worried as to how I could manage to have his ceiling repaired.

Some weeks later, I noticed his kitchen ceiling had been beautifully replaced! I asked him who had paid for the work to be done and he replied, "My insurance!"

God had again intervened for me! Praise the Lord! All these blessings came as a result of God's provision of the apartment which, at first I disliked, but which I came to accept as God's wise choice for me and my family. If I had turned down this offer of accommodation, all of these other blessings would not have followed.

When we obey God, He blesses us abundantly. Because of my being in God's will and location, I was released for His purposes and was ready to use my gifts of evangelism, Bible teaching and hospitality to reach out to people of many different nationalities.

Seed of a Dandelion

To IMPROVE MY ENGLISH SPEAKING skills, I enrolled in an English language class being offered at a city college. A Chinese lady and I were together in the same class when one day I asked her whether she had ever heard of Jesus. Then I enquired about her knowledge of God and questioned her about who she thought created the universe. She was unable to give a response to those questions other than saying that she did not know.

I explained that, having these questions answered was much more important than learning English. I volunteered to share my experience of God with her and her husband and invited them to my home for a Korean meal. I told her how much I enjoyed cooking for visitors.

Before we ate, I prayed and gave God thanks for our food. The Chinese couple asked me why I prayed before the meal and I had an opportunity to explain. I emphasized that God created all our food. I asked them "Who do you think created the amazing variety of plants and animals we eat?

I wanted the couple to look beyond themselves and their families and realize that there is a God who is real and worthy of our worship. They did not have an answer so I shared scripture from the first chapter of Genesis. The couple had never heard about the Bible but they began to accept and believe in God as their Creator. As we ate together, I told them that there was so much more to learn about God and Jesus, His son, and encouraged them to come again to my home for a Bible study.

Every Saturday, I cooked Korean food and taught from the Bible to my Chinese friends. We enjoyed great times of food and fellowship and they believed more and more of the Bible. They invited other couples and many were added to our meeting on a regular basis. Our new friends had all come from China on educational scholarships to study at the doctorate level at Universities in Edinburgh. God used the Chinese lady from the English class to bring over fifteen new believers to know the Lord.

I was busily engaged with teaching the Bible to my Chinese friends when God told Paul, on four separate occasions to go to Urumchi, Beijing, Shanghai, and Harbin and intercede for the revival of those cities. However, Paul was puzzled as he did not know anyone in China, but in hindsight God had already prepared the way for him to fulfil this mission.

It happened that among my Chinese friends who attended the Bible meetings were four from those four cities! For each of Paul's trips, God used my Chinese friends to connect Paul with the people in their respective home towns. They helped him with his day-to-day needs during his stay.

Therefore, God not only brought salvation to my Chinese friends but also used them for His plan for their cities in China. Nothing is a coincidence! Everything was part of God's divine connections!

Eventually the Chinese students completed their doctorates and I bade them farewell as they accepted good jobs and moved to positions in Australia, Canada, the United States, Norway and China. They extended invitations for me to visit them if I ever had the opportunity to do so. So God's promise that I would minister to and bless all nations was beginning to be fulfilled. The Lord enabled me to accept the invitations.

Faith is the assurance of things hoped for, the conviction of things not seen. (Hebrews 11:1)

Without faith it is impossible to please Him. (Hebrews 11:6)

JEHOVAH JIREH—THE PROVIDER

Chinese Bible Study Group

Divine Connections in Uganda

S EVERAL YEARS LATER, I MOVED to a large house where my
Wednesday Bible Study continued. Paul and his family
regularly attended these meetings and on one particular evening
they brought a guest named Arnold, who was a Ugandan pastor
living in England. He gave his testimony which did not conclude
until midnight.

Pastor Arnold decided to stay overnight as we had ample
room and after the other prayer group members had left, he said,
"God showed me this house and you, a Korean lady, two months
ago." He continued, "This house is a house of prayer, a house of
salvation, a house of blessing and a house filled with the presence
of God."

Pastor Arnold went on to explain that two months earlier, he
had been shown a vision of me in my house, but dismissed it. He
was wondering why God would show him, as an African man, a
Korean lady. He forgot all about it until he sat on the sofa in my
home on the night of the prayer meeting! God reminded him of
the vision and told him, "This is the house and this is the lady."

Arnold realized that God had brought him to Edinburgh,
not only to visit Paul's family, but expressly to meet me. The next
morning Arnold said, "God has told me that you need to go to
Uganda to attend a conference."

This was unexpected and surprising, so I replied, "I have never
thought about going to Africa and I don't have sufficient finance
for a trip like that." Arnold explained that God said that He had
already provided the finance for me and asked that I should trust
and obey Him. So that being the case, I decided that I must follow
God's leading and make the trip to Uganda.

After Arnold had delivered this message, he returned to his

home in England. A few weeks later, he called me to say that ten English people were going to accompany him to Uganda. He asked me to send my fare contribution so that he could buy us group tickets. I replied that I had not yet received sufficient finance from God, but when God provided, I would make my own travel arrangements. I did not want the other people in the group to delay in booking tickets for my sake. I was happy to travel separately once God had provided the finance I needed for my ticket.

The next day, I unexpectedly received a check for a large sum of money and surprisingly it was for more than ten times the amount of the ticket price to Uganda! Prior to this incident, I had supported myself from my own funds. Now my funds were exhausted and I was totally dependent on God for my financial income. This was the start of living by faith in The Provider. This financial miracle re-affirmed my trust in God's ability to supply all my needs.

God faithfully provided ample funds for my trip and I went to Uganda to the two weeks long Africamp Fasting and Prayer Conference.

Paul had been the first foreign speaker at the original Africamp meeting years earlier. God sent him to Uganda to share the exciting news about God's work in the Korean church. He explained at the meeting the concept of the Korean Prayer Mountains, taught about fasting prayer and shared some of my story. A Ugandan lady, Florence, was fascinated upon hearing of the experiences of Emily Chang and prayed a heartfelt prayer that she would meet me sometime in the future.

When I was attending the conference in Uganda, our main speaker was Cindy Jacobs, the author of 'Possessing the Gates of the Enemy.' I was inspired by her preaching and it was an immense blessing to be involved in that time of anointing. There were many other high profile speakers from all over the world who came to share about God's work in their own home countries. I thanked God for the opportunity to be seeking Him together in an international gathering with many Ugandan Christian supporters.

While we were in Uganda, the ten English people from Arnold's group and I visited the home of a Ugandan lady named Florence, who was Pastor Arnold's sister. She herself was the wife of a pastor, with a family of eight children and, as well, caring for many orphaned and needy children. It so happened, I discovered later, that she was the same Florence who had prayed to meet me those years before at the Africamp meeting!

Each day, Florence and her husband, Pastor Enos, led the children in Spirit-anointed devotions of prayer, worship and Bible study. Even the very youngest could pray and praise God and others would prophesy. Their home resounded with preaching, prayers, praises and glory to God all the time! While I was there with them, the days were like days of heaven upon earth.

Florence and her family lived by faith. They were poor people financially, but rich in faith and trust toward God. They lived in a rented house and the rent for the house was due on the tenth day of every month. It was often a struggle to meet this deadline. God revealed to Florence, a few days before my visit that, "This month, on the 11th of January, someone will give you the rent money you need."

On the morning of that exact date while I was visiting Florence's home, the Holy Spirit prompted me to give one hundred pounds to her without my knowing that she needed it. She was overjoyed, and told me that the money was the exact amount needed for her rent! She was delighted that God's promise was fulfilled through me. The Bible tells us:

But whoever has this world's goods, and sees his brother in need, and shuts up his heart from him, how does the love of God abide in him? *(1 John 3:17)*

I was moved by the Holy Spirit to put some more money into the bank for her future needs. But Florence had never had enough money for the deposit to open a bank account. So I went with her to the bank and opened an account for her, supplying the deposit she needed. The next day one of the English men in our group asked Florence, "Do you have a bank account?" "Yes!" She replied with great delight and excitement. So he promised to send money for the purpose of giving one of her children a good education.

After one week of prayer and fasting, I was keen to begin cooking my own food in order to build up some strength. I needed to do this as I was planning a trip to Israel soon after leaving Uganda. So I purchased a little portable electric cooking stove and a pot. I later discovered that Florence's cooker had broken down and she had been unable to have it repaired or afford to buy a new one. But the Lord, knowing of her situation, prompted me to leave the cooker and cooking pan for her. It was just what was required for Florence and her family and fulfilled a promise that God had given to her that He would provide a new cooker. Florence and her family were such a large group with many mouths to feed, so this gift was soon put to good use.

It is so wonderful that God is concerned with every detail of our lives, even the basic needs in life like a kitchen cooker! Florence explained to me that the cooker I gave her was an exact copy of the model she had owned previously. She was overwhelmed by God's care and attention.

I had also brought some clothing and personal belongings with me to Uganda for my own use and these I shared with her too, leaving almost everything to her family including an expensive camera and some cash. The Lord touched my heart when I saw the poverty of these needy people.

Florence wept many tears of gratitude and said to me "From today I will intercede in prayer for you each day until the day I die!" That was more than ten years ago, and she still keeps her promise today. God had sent me on an incredible journey to Uganda and it had led to many blessings for me and my new friend and sister, Florence.

Two months after visiting Uganda, I called Florence at her church office. I asked her whether her rent had been paid for the past two months as I was personally curious as to how God had provided. "Nobody has helped us." she replied sorrowfully, "The landlord is likely to evict us."

When I heard this, I felt that it was God who had prompted me to call and discover her need. I offered to help so I sent her two months' rent and the Lord graciously enabled me to send another one thousand pounds to Florence's bank account for her to buy a home telephone line, a fax machine and a refrigerator. I also asked the members of my prayer group to help financially support her by sending two hundred pounds per month for her rent and bills. Some from the prayer group agreed to join me in that undertaking and this commitment continues today.

So while God enables us to support Florence materially, she faithfully supports us spiritually. We bless each other in a divine connection arranged by God. It is an example of what God can do when we trust Him totally!

The following verses remind us, that if we claim to be people of God, then we shall have a heart for the poor.

He who oppresses the poor reproaches his Maker, but he who honors Him has mercy on the needy. (Proverbs 14:31)

He who has pity on the poor lends to the Lord, and he will pay back what he has given. (Proverbs 19:17)

Emily and Florence in Uganda

The Sovereignty of God

*S*OON AFTER RETURNING FROM THE Africamp conference, I
received a letter from the conference leader. He sent me an
invitation to attend again the following year. He wanted me to
lecture on world mission to students at the missionary training
course at one of the seminars.

I thought about this invitation, but considered that, as there
were so many other special speakers attending the conference, it
was unnecessary for me to make the journey from Scotland to
Uganda for one session. I could see from the written information
about the camp that there would be other speakers who could
easily lead sessions on world mission. I put the letter to one side
and forgot about it, believing that it was not really a priority.

I did not tell the conference organizers what I was thinking
straight away because I presumed that they would guess that
the delay in answering meant that I was unable to attend. The
conference was a fortnight's duration so the organizers began
without me, all the while assuming that I would be coming just
prior to my lecture.

The first week went by, and I remained in Scotland. On the
Monday of the second week I made a telephone call to Uganda to
let people know that I would not be attending.

But they responded by saying: "We have been praying for you
and waiting expectantly for you to arrive. You must come!"

I was then convinced that it was God's will for me to go, so the
next day, in obedience, I flew out to the conference in Uganda.

On the day of my arrival in Kampala, Uganda, I heard the
sad news that the mother of my friend Florence had died. So
Florence had very mixed emotions that day: sorrow at the loss of

her mother, but joy in being re-united with me again. My arrival in some way helped to reduce her emotional pain.

I stayed at Florence's home in Kampala, and on Friday, the last day of the conference, I gave my lecture on world mission to the students. As I looked out over the crowd I could see just one white face in the midst of about fifty African students. It was a young man called Joseph who I later discovered, had recently graduated in science from a University in England. Joseph and I were about to experience another of God's divine connections.

This is the background for Joseph's presence at the conference. I came to know his story after delivering my single lecture in Uganda.

Joseph had accepted Christ as his Savior when a Jamaican student at his university had witnessed to him. This Jamaican student introduced Joseph to an African church before returning to Jamaica. Through this church Joseph had become close friends with many Africans. After graduation, one of his friends suggested that he spend some time in Africa before he sought employment. So he had gone to Kenya for a time, and whilst there his friend suggested that he attend the Africamp Conference in Uganda.

The night before he was due to leave for Uganda, God gave Joseph a vision of a lady wearing a dress with a pattern of roses. At the time of the vision, he did not understand why God would show him a lady with such a dress. He then heard the audible voice of God saying, "You will meet her in Kampala."

This was the first time he had actually experienced a vision and had heard the audible voice of God.

On his arrival at the conference in the first week, he searched and searched for the lady in the rose-patterned dress, but he did not see a woman that matched the image that he had been given in his vision. He kept searching each day for that woman but finally gave up on Thursday about twelve days into the conference. He doubted the vision and wondered whether it really had been from God.

Joseph had been attending the lectures on the topic of intercession throughout the week. However, on the Friday, the classroom was altered unexpectedly and Joseph was unable to find the new location for the seminar. Sensing that Joseph was at a loss, a friend managed to persuade him to join the lecture on world mission. This was my session and that day I had chosen to wear a suit with an elaborately patterned floral dress.

As the session got underway, Joseph became entranced by the message, for up until now he had not received any teaching about world mission. He had a burning desire to discuss the ideas presented in my lecture and to ask some further questions. So while I was teaching, he prayed, "Lord, give me the opportunity to speak with this lecturer."

After the lecture, God answered his prayer. It was in fact I who approached Joseph because I detected during the meeting God revealing that there was to be a very special calling for this person in the future of which he was yet unaware and there was much he had to learn in the area of world mission.

While we spoke together, Joseph suddenly recognized the dress I was wearing, and shouted out, "It's you!" He then explained about the vision he had seen of me in that particular dress.

We talked for several hours about God and life in service to Him and I shared more of my testimony. After this, we went to Florence's home and asked her to intercede for him in prayer concerning God's plan for his future. After that, we went to a Chinese restaurant for a meal. For Joseph it had been an amazing day. He had been fed spiritually, been refreshed and was now enjoying a generous and richly varied meal. This was a great blessing as he had not been able to eat properly in Uganda for two weeks! It was made all the more special because it came as a result of meeting someone he had seen in a vision from God. It was certainly a day that he would never forget!

Joseph returned to Kenya after the Africamp conference finished, and I returned to my home in Scotland. Later, he sent me a letter expressing his thanks for an amazing experience. He asked the Lord why He had given him a vision of me and why God had arranged for us to meet. He knew it must be significant and wanted to understand God's intention. He then felt God say, "I want you to be a missionary in North Korea."

He was certain that this was from God, but it was a shock and a little confusing because he never planned to be a missionary and had never heard of North Korea! Then he felt God say "I will begin to prepare you in six months' time."

He would never have even imagined that this was God's intention for our meeting. There was a conflict in his mind. He was filled with doubts and said, "No. I don't want to be a missionary because I have been a Christian for only two years and have never been taught about mission apart from the one lecture given by Emily!" Then he closed his ears and his heart to God's voice. But the Lord persisted and said to him, "She will help you." However, he continued to resist the word of the Lord. Like Jonah in the Bible, he tried to escape.

Joseph returned to England after all this and, to avoid the call to the mission field, tried to get a job. However, all his applications for employment were rejected. Then he applied for a PhD course in science, but that was also rejected.

At the end of six months, Joseph attended a prayer meeting in Kent, England and found that a large number of Koreans were also there. The next day, he went to the library and found a stray book next to the computer he was using. The book was about soils, but he knew in his spirit that if he opened it, the page would be about North Korea. He opened the book and the page opened exactly at a page entitled 'The Soils of North Korea.' Not only that, he overheard apparently casual conversations of strangers on the street and discovered that the topic was North Korea.

He even received an email from his friend in the United States stating that North Korea needed missionaries! Everywhere he went it seemed that North Korea was being pressed upon him.

Finally, he went to a prayer meeting and heard an Indian pastor tell him: "When I intercede for you, my tongue says, "Send to Korea. Send to Korea!"

At this point, Joseph submitted to God and called me. He explained that he had been reluctant to tell me all his experiences where God had been confirming that he should be a missionary in North Korea. It was only after the Indian pastor had directly said, 'Send to Korea' that he knew he needed to surrender to God's will. He knew that I would help him and that God had connected us for a reason.

So I invited Joseph to my home and he came to visit. I was very happy to help him when I heard of all the ways in which God had been speaking to him and confirming his special calling. I started to pray for him and then I suggested he should make a visit to South Korea to find out about the country and receive information about North Korea because of his total ignorance about that country. He agreed, but had no funds available. So I helped him by making arrangements with Korean friends to offer him the support that he needed.

The pastor of his church in Kent found it hard to accept that Joseph had a missionary calling to North Korea because of his inexperience. So Joseph invited me to visit his pastor in Kent and I was able to convince him that the call was genuine.

I went to Kent during a mission week at his church. Several international speakers were there including an American, an

Italian and an Indian. They evangelized for a week and won souls for Christ.

On the Saturday, they held a party to which many were invited, including all the new converts. I went to the party and sat down next to the speakers and pastors to eat my meal. A visiting Church of England leader who was sitting next to me asked me questions so I showed him a short version of my testimony on paper. The reason I carried a brief version of my testimony was because people were always asking about my life and why I had left Korea for Scotland. After reading the testimony, he was impressed and said, "Can you preach at my church tomorrow morning?" I agreed without hesitation. So Joseph and I went to this church where I preached at the morning service.

After that, we then returned to Joseph's church where the service was still in progress. The Italian pastor was preaching, and during his preaching the Holy Spirit came upon him and he prophesied over Joseph!

"The Lord is sending you to North Korea. There will be planting involved with churches. In a vision I can see great fear on your face as you are surrounded by people who are clinging onto you. But these people are Christians and will help you. You will become involved with twenty six underground churches. This movement will spread to a neighboring country and then to another country."

After that, he continued to prophesy saying to me, "You have made big steps in the past. You have a power and glory through Christ of which you don't know. People will be blessed through you wherever you go. The Lord has given you power to do things. People will be filled with the Spirit through you. You are very sensitive to the Holy Spirit and a very, very powerful ambassador for Christ."

Joseph's pastor who was conducting the meeting then stood and announced, "At this evening's service, Emily will speak!"

He declared this despite knowing that an Indian pastor was the speaker planned for that evening service! We must be prepared to accept changes when we give control to the Holy Spirit.

After I spoke at the evening service, the pastor called Joseph to the front with the elders and other pastors. They prayed and laid hands on him and publicly acknowledged him as a missionary to North Korea!

How wonderfully God worked in His sovereign power and grace! The reason I went to his church was to convince his pastor, but the Holy Spirit did all the work, without me having to speak a word.

"I will pour out My Spirit on all flesh; your sons and your daughters shall prophesy, your old men shall dream dreams, your young men shall see visions." (Joel 2:28)

JEHOVAH EL ROI—THE GOD OF VISION

Lecturing to Ugandan missionary students

CHAPTER 3

Seeds and Shoots

Meeting Key People

*E*VENTUALLY, JOSEPH WENT TO SOUTH Korea. I knew it was right for me to obey God in assisting him until he had accomplished the work that God had called him to do. Before he left, I prayed that he might meet the right person to aid him with his training for mission in North Korea. God led me to Hyung Ko, a Korean worship leader in Seoul, South Korea with a heart for North Korea. I believed that he would be instrumental in enabling Joseph to complete his mission. So Joseph was able to connect with that worship leader and gain important insights for his journey into North Korea.

Incidentally, the day after Joseph and Hyung met, Pastor Ross who is the head of a training school for North Korea missions in Canada was visiting Seoul for only two days to attend a wedding. During those two days, he happened to phone the worship leader Hyung just to greet him as a co-worker for North Korea missions. When Hyung told Pastor Ross about Joseph and his amazing calling for North Korea over the phone, Pastor Ross was eager to make his acquaintance, regardless of his tight schedule in Korea. So the three, one from the United Kingdom, one from Korea, and one from the United States who had one common calling to be missionaries for North Korea, were gathered in one place by God's divine connections.

Upon hearing Joseph's testimony, and how miraculously God had called him, Pastor Ross immediately accepted Joseph for training.

Joseph was aware that he needed six thousand dollars for his Training School fees, including outreach costs in China, and his flight ticket to Canada to go to the North Korean mission school.

He wondered how he would come by this amount of money, but I encouraged him and said, "When you say 'Yes' to God and obey Him, then He will provide for your needs!"

I prayed about this matter and felt that God wanted us to go to a Korean Church in New Jersey, in the United States. The Holy Spirit revealed to me that there, the necessary fees for Joseph's training would be raised. So, despite not having any money, I booked two flight tickets to Canada via New York. We were due to leave on the Saturday, and up until Thursday there was still no money! Joseph telephoned me from London wondering at which airport we would be meeting. Knowing that we had not yet paid for the tickets, but having the faith that God would provide, I replied confidently, "Heathrow Airport."

I contacted the travel agents with whom I had booked the

flights saying, "Please do not cancel the reservations; I will pay tomorrow, on Friday." This I promised by faith. I had no idea where the money would come from, but I knew God would provide.

On that Thursday evening, Joseph telephoned again to say that a man had promised to deposit a sizeable sum of money into his bank account on the following day, which was Friday. This money would cover the price of the tickets exactly. So we paid the travel agent as I had promised, on Friday, and collected the tickets!

I contacted the Korean church in New Jersey to advise that we were coming in two days' time. I had visited this church twice before to share my testimony and had previously preached to the congregation. On our arrival, the pastor's wife queried our giving such short notice. In the car en route to her home, I explained about God's provision of the funds at the last minute and Joseph's unique calling and testimony.

At the pastor's home, his wife described Joseph's circumstances and his need of provision for his training. The pastor was concerned and asked, "How will you get this large sum of money in just one week?" "One week is long enough for God to provide." I replied. I knew in my heart that God was going to use this pastor's church to provide the money for Joseph's needs, as the Holy Spirit had revealed this before we had made the journey.

On Sunday, at the service, the pastor explained our visit and the fact that this time I was accompanied by a special guest who had been given a missionary call to North Korea and whose testimony the congregation would hear on Wednesday.

On Wednesday evening, Joseph testified in the church, and the people wept freely when they heard of his calling and the situation in North Korea. They gave a generous offering which covered his mission training fees. We were due to leave on the following afternoon when a man invited us for breakfast. He gave Joseph an envelope containing enough cash for his outreach to

China! God's amazing grace is inexpressible when we trust Him! He keeps His promises. He is Jehovah Jireh the Provider. We flew from New York to Vancouver to stay overnight and then go to the mission school the following day. A pastor friend who lives in Vancouver arranged for me to stay with a lady whose ministry was that of a prophetic intercessor. As a hotel employee, she believed that I would be better accommodated at her place of work. So she asked the manager whether a room could be provided free of charge for a friend. The owner agreed and enquired about the friend's occupation. The lady-intercessor did not know much at all about me, but she felt her lips forming the word "missionary" She wondered why she had said this, and then immediately the Holy Spirit spoke to her saying: "You are right. She is a prophetic intercessory missionary. Do not accommodate her in the hotel but let her stay at your home. You will be blessed and she will tell you amazing stories."

So Joseph, who was included in her invitation, and I, arrived at her house at midnight. The first words she spoke to me were, "Tell me amazing stories!" So I told her one of the stories involving Joseph's calling. Again, God had provided for us in a miraculous way and we were able to stay with this lady and encourage her in her faith by telling her about all the wonderful things that God had been doing.

Joseph learned much during his training in Canada that was immensely useful for his calling to North Korea. He met many Korean people during this time and his love for the country intensified. God gave him a new level of compassion for people who so needed to hear the gospel.

After completing the course in Canada, God led Joseph to the border of North Korea and China for further practical training, preparing him for missionary work in North Korea. God was leading him through a journey of faith and guiding him all the way, making miraculous provision for his every need. I was the means by which God supported him in this journey and at each twist and turn I had faith that God would do what was necessary to make it possible for Joseph to fulfil his calling.

It is wonderful to reflect how God gave a vision to an English man while he was in Kenya which led him to go to Uganda to meet a Korean lady from Scotland.

He was then led to go to Korea to meet an American mission leader, and then onto the United States to meet with a Korean church there. Finally he travelled to Canada and China to train for mission before going to North Korea.

God uses people of all nationalities and backgrounds in his glorious plan of salvation. To God be all the glory!

JEHOVAH ELSHADDAI—MY ALL SUFFICIENT GOD

From Uganda Leading To Germany

*B*ACK IN 2000, I HAD taken the leader of the conference in Uganda to Korea to see our Prayer Mountains and churches there. He asked me to speak at Africamp 2001 about the Korean Prayer Mountains and share my testimony. Joseph also testified to God's amazing arrangement of the right connections with key people to fulfil His purpose in his life and the fact that his faith journey had begun in Uganda gave him all the more reason to speak at the conference.

At this particular conference, the Ugandan 'Prayer Mountain for all Nations' was established. About a thousand people attended, including approximately fifty representatives from every country in Europe. Among them were two hundred German-speaking people from Austria, Switzerland and Germany itself.

When I spoke of the Korean church, Prayer Mountains and my personal testimony, the people were amazed at the wonderful things God had done. A pastor from Germany, Berthold Klein, was deeply moved by my faith. He was so affected that he was unable to speak for five hours! God directed him to pass his name card to me with his contact details. As he approached, I was praying in my seat, so he quietly put his card in the pages of my Bible and went away without my realizing what had happened.

Following my personal prayer time, a pastor, his wife and a translator knelt down and asked me to pray for them to receive an anointing of faith and obedience. Then later more German people came to me for this blessing.

The power of the Holy Spirit's anointing was such that many people, particularly the Germans, were so influenced by my testimony that they were hungering for a deeper experience of the reality of the Holy Spirit in their own lives.

A man who was a German publisher came to meet me and during the course of our conversation he asked me the question, "Why don't you write a book?" "I would rather not." was my reply. Previously, many other people had made similar suggestions, but I had always returned this negative answer.

"Don't hide what God has done in your life." he responded. I had always thought that unless God specifically told me to write a book, I would not do it. However, this rebuke gave me something to think upon and pray about, so I spent some time seeking the Lord. Afterwards, I came to believe that it was right to consider writing a book about my life with God. Although still very dubious and hesitant, it was still some time before I began to record my story.

Perhaps I would have let the challenge go except that years later, in Los Angeles, I received a reminder. I was at a prayer meeting for that city when the leader of the meeting, Jean Darnall, a well-known speaker and intercessor predicted without knowing anything about me, that through my book, God's ministry would be enlarged! When I questioned her about which book she meant, she said "Your testimony." I was taken aback and amazed by God's specific direction given through a person that I had only just met.

After the Africamp conference, I was to fly home from Kampala, Uganda via Amsterdam. But there were yet more connections to be made.

Before he left for the airport, Bethold Klein, the German pastor who had placed his name card in my Bible was desperate to see me again. As no one knew of my whereabouts, he prayed that he might meet me but was still unable to locate me at the conference.

On his arrival at Kampala Airport, he believed that now it would be impossible to catch up with me. So when he saw me arrive at the airport he shouted, "She's coming! She's coming!" And he and a group of others broke into spontaneous applause! It was wonderful to discover that so many German people from the conference were on my flight to Amsterdam! There was going to be yet more time to be devoted to ministry.

The Holy Spirit revealed to Karin, Pastor Klein's wife that she and her husband were going to be seated next to me on that flight. There were more than two hundred passengers, so there appeared to be little chance of that allocation happening. But we were all delighted when it occurred! God arranges surprises for us which demonstrate His great attention to detail!

During the flight, we were able to share our testimonies more fully and pray for each other. Then several of the German people came across to where I was sitting and knelt in the aisle to receive prayer. I suggested we continue praying once we had landed in Amsterdam so as not to inconvenience the flight attendants on the plane!

At Amsterdam airport, many pastors gave me details of their names and addresses and invited me to Germany. I felt in my spirit that God would send me there one day. During my prayer for those dear people, I also rejoiced that many German pastors had humbled themselves to ask for prayer. I recalled the Scripture from

2 Chronicles 7:14, "If My people who are called by My name humble themselves and pray, and seek My face, and turn from their wicked ways, then I will hear from heaven, will forgive their sin, and will heal their land."

The German people from the conference really obeyed the terms of that Scripture. They hungered and thirsted for God to come afresh with a new anointing of His Holy Spirit. This is the only path to true revival in the churches and in the nations. If we would meet God's conditions and humble ourselves, then God will keep His promise and heal our land!

Two months later, I received an e-mail from a lady unknown to me called Nancy, who lived in Houston, Texas in the United States. In her correspondence, she introduced herself and mentioned that she had prayed for Germany for ten years shedding many tears as she did so. Now it was time God told her to actually travel to Germany herself but she knew no-one in that country and had never been to Europe. So she was wondering how she would be able to obey this command to go to Germany in person.

One morning, a Texan friend of mine, Tom, who also knew Nancy, received a clear message from the Lord: "Connect Nancy with Emily." That was how Nancy was given my e-mail address. I replied to Nancy's e-mail informing her of the many connections I had in Germany after attending the conference in Uganda. At my reply, she was able to relax, knowing that there were people who would welcome her.

So God had been, even then, paving the way for us to travel to this country together and because of this, I invited Nancy to visit me in Scotland. On June 2nd, 2001, Nancy came to my home.

I felt that the key person to be involved with us should be Pastor Klein, so I contacted him and prepared him for the arrival of Nancy and myself in Germany. He understood that this was the prompting of the Lord. He explained that he planned an intercession conference lasting for ten days at Weil Am Rheine in Germany. It would be commencing on June 6th. "I have invited three women speakers from Uganda." he said. "But if you and Nancy can come too, it will be perfect." After we talked, he telephoned Nancy in America to welcome her to his country in advance. So Nancy and I made plans to fly to Germany on June 5th, 2001.

JEHOVAH EL GIBBOR—THE MIGHTY GOD

Sharing my testimony at Africamp

Karin and Berthold Klein

Inner Healing Ministry and God's Care

*G*OD HAD FAITHFULLY PROVIDED FINANCE on so many occasions for my ministry abroad. I obeyed God and went wherever He sent me. Although I was at that time concerned about my general living costs, I did not prioritize these expenses, but put God's kingdom first. *Matthew 6:33 states 'But seek first the kingdom of God and His righteousness, and all these things shall be added to you.' I trusted this promise.*

On June 4th of that same year, I received a notice which stated that unless I settled unpaid rent within one month, I would be forced to vacate my home. I felt deeply depressed and became very upset and fearful about this situation. I wondered how I would raise the fund I needed by the July 3rd, especially when God was leading me to Germany. How could I justify going with Nancy, having encountered all this hardship and knowing I had much to resolve financially? I surrendered this situation into God's hands and focused on the things He had called me to do.

Even though Nancy did not have spare money for herself, God had asked her before she left the United States to give me two envelopes containing gifts of money. One contained two hundred dollars for my plane ticket to Germany, and the other one a personal gift of three hundred dollars! Without her knowing about my financial difficulty, the Lord had directed her to provide for my trip to Germany.

So I decided I would obey God and go with Nancy trusting that it was God who would deal with all my other issues. We went to the travel agency, but discovered that two hundred dollars would only pay for a one-way ticket. God had allowed the necessary funds for a one-way ticket only. So I purchased exactly that!

God was testing me yet again and I had to trust that there was a divine plan to bring me home and to resolve all of my financial problems. By faith I left all these matters in God's hands. I thought of the words of a song I often sing:

Father I place into Your hands
the things that I can't do,
Father I place into Your hands
the times that I've been through.
Father I place into Your hands
the way that I should go.
For I know, I always can trust You.

Father I want to be with You,
and do the things You do.
Father I want to speak the words,
that You are speaking too.
Father I want to love the ones,
that You will draw to You
For I know, that I am one with You.
(Jenny Hewer, 1975)

We travelled to Germany the following day. Pastor Klein had arranged accommodation for us throughout the conference at the home of Marian, a Swiss lady. We slept that first night in Germany at her home and the next morning she explained that the Lord had spoken to her during the night. He had told her to give me one hundred Deutschmarks (the equivalent of fifty dollars). Marian had no knowledge of my financial situation, but God had chosen her to bestow blessing upon me.

One of the speakers at the conference in Weil am Rheine was a powerful intercessor from Uganda Africa. She was an orphan girl whom we had previously met in Uganda. God had also directed her during the previous night to pass one hundred Deutschmarks on to me and she wondered about the reason for this. She was under the impression that I was rich, so she asked God why such a poor person as herself should give to the rich a small sum of money! God spoke to her saying "Give it to Emily. It will be a blessing to you and to her."

So she approached me during the lunch break of the conference and said, "Emily, a very strange thing happened last night. God asked me to give you one hundred Deutschmarks but I thought you to be a wealthy woman. Why would God ask me, a poor orphan, to give you, a rich woman, a small sum of money?"

I told her that, to the contrary, I was far from being rich and was struggling financially. I suggested that she should trust and obey God. In this way God was able to demonstrate to me, even within the first day of my stay in Germany, that He was honoring my trust and that He was completely faithful. Later on another person also gave me a gift of the same amount. I came to Germany with an empty wallet but it was God who provided for me throughout the trip.

During the first meeting of the conference, despite there being five women speakers to be introduced, the convener, Pastor Klein, spent most of the time explaining to the listeners of our meeting in Uganda and how he had been amazed at the things that God had done in my life. He then asked me to begin to speak and pray to open the meeting.

During the conference, Nancy and I were used miraculously for the inner healing of many people who had been tormented by abuse. I came to a realisation of why Nancy had been linked with me in ministry at this time. She had been sexually abused several times since early childhood, but had not spoken about this to people at home in the United States.

God directed her to speak of her experiences while in Europe and tell His people about the need for forgiveness, repentance and reconciliation. So Nancy obeyed God and shared with the people at the conference about her past sexual abuse and how it had affected her. Nancy spoke lovingly about the need to forgive. To my great surprise many people came for counselling and prayer. Up until then, I had no idea of the widespread nature of this abuse.

As people came forward to share and to pray, one lady told of her abuse at the age of fourteen by a Korean man in Switzerland. Because of this traumatic experience, she had been unable to forgive him and her life had been blighted by a spirit of bitterness. After she heard Nancy's story and her teaching concerning the need to forgive, she realized that she needed ministry to release her anger and bitterness. She came to me crying and asking for help. She asked me to represent her abuser so that forgiveness could enter her heart. I stood as proxy for the man, and with tears, asked for her forgiveness for the abuse she had suffered. She forgave him.

Then I, (in his place) forgave her for her bitter hatred. She was gloriously delivered and healed and was visibly filled with joy in the Spirit. It was God who had released her from the sorrow and anger that she had carried for over thirty years!

Another instance arose when God led me to a young man who needed deliverance and healing. He revealed that when he was fifteen years old, his father, an oil company executive, had taken him to Korea and paid for him to have sex with a prostitute. The boy was cruel to the prostitute, and he was himself taken over by an evil spirit of lust which had held him in bondage for many years.

I counselled him, and stood as proxy for the Korean prostitute. He forgave her (me) and I forgave him for his mistreatment of the prostitute. He was then fully released from his bondage. He told me that I had changed his life and he hugged me and wailed and cried. The miracle of God's pardoning grace!

A further story emerged from this man. He had been struggling to obey God's call to move to the United States. He explained that God had told him thirteen times to move there. The man himself was American but his wife was German and they had six children. They lacked financial resources and he didn't have the boldness or the confidence to leave Germany. However, he was touched by my testimony about how God had originally asked me to leave Korea, without my children. He admitted that it was a struggle to obey God even though God had not asked him to part with his children. God was only asking him to relocate with his family to the United States.

He immediately decided in his heart to obey God even though it would not be easy. He told me that meeting me had changed his life. I praised God for His transforming power.

Shortly after, the man's family moved in obedience to the United States. I was encouraged by the amazing way that God was using me in Germany and could see that He had a specific plan to bless that country through the ministry of forgiveness.

God is Amazing!

These cases provide clear evidence of the power of forgiveness. God's compassionate heart extends to every person from every corner of the globe. He uses people of all nationalities to minister to others and bring healing.

God made a divine connection between Nancy from America and myself, a Korean from Scotland, and a Swiss person living in Germany. Through this, we all experienced that one of the greatest powers in the Universe is the power to forgive through the grace of our loving Lord.

JEHOVAH MEKADSHI—THE LORD MY SANCTIFIER

Only a Little Spaghetti and Salt

*A*FTER GIVING MY TESTIMONY AT the conference in Germany, I was approached by a woman called Katharina, a teacher of English at a German private high school. Katharina was a Christian concerned that her students should know more about the living Lord. She had a request that I address her class for an hour, giving the students a Christian message. I was pleased to be able to do this.

During my visit to Katharina's school, I taught her class a Christian song in Korean. This immediately caught their attention and they were soon singing with enthusiasm, "Bless the Lord O my soul!" I could then translate the words from Korean, and relate them to their Biblical source in *Psalm 103:1 Bless the Lord, o my soul: and all that is within me bless His holy name.*

I preached to the class a simple message on the choice between two ways to live in life, the right way and the wrong way. The right way is to follow Jesus and obey Him. The wrong way is to live your life without God.

Katharina thanked me for sharing and the children were touched by this powerful message. I reminded them never to forget what had been taught that day concerning the right way to live with God at the center of your life.

When I had finished teaching the class, it was lunch time and Katharina had another appointment. This meant that she was unable to show me to my accommodation. Katharina suggested she accompany me to the nearby residence of a young man called David, a fifth year student in Theological College whom I had met previously and had prayed for on the first day of the conference. During that time, the Holy Spirit prompted me to help him but

I did not know at that time how or why. Now God had given me another opportunity to meet with him to discover His purpose.

David had in fact missed hearing my testimony at the conference in Weil am Rheine but now, on this visit, I was able to give him a brief written copy of some of the highlights of my testimony.

The next day, David explained that two years ago he had been given a dream which unfolded as a striking drama. He described his dream to me. "In my dream an oriental lady gave me her written testimony. Then she and I went to Israel and prayed together at the Sea of Galilee. We also attended a wedding in Scotland in a beautiful church. After that, we flew to Korea as business class passengers. We then travelled to Bangladesh and Thailand. As the dream closed I saw this same lady receiving a large crown in heaven, and a voice saying 'This crown is your reward for the many souls who were saved as a result of reading your book of testimony!"

I was amazed when he recounted his dream to me. It was astounding to hear that God had spoken of me to him two years earlier even though we had never previously met! It was encouraging to know that my book of testimony would bring many people to God.

During my time at David's house, I became very hungry, but the only food David had was a small packet of spaghetti and some salt! I asked him about his small supply of food. He explained that he had enough money to support himself, but he also used his money to support seven theology students in the Philippines. The only way he could save money was by not purchasing food.

Upon hearing this, I felt that David was so precious to God and gave him one hundred Deutschmarks from the three hundred I had received, with the instruction that he was to use it only for buying food.

We decided to go to the supermarket to purchase supplies including some tasty pasta sauce.

We came home and cooked a meal with spaghetti and the sauce. "Wow!" exclaimed David, "With that sauce it is so delicious!" Previously, he had only eaten boiled spaghetti with salt!

When the conference was over, David invited Nancy and me to accompany him to his parents' home near Munich. We had a time of prayer during which we prayed for his family who were away at the time.

Playing the piano was the way in which David worshipped the Lord. He cried and interceded for his country praying, "Forgive Germany, save Germany please, Lord."

He was weeping uncontrollably for his country.

2 Chronicles 7:14 says "If My people who are called by My name will humble themselves, and pray and seek My face, and turn from their wicked ways, then I will hear from heaven, and will forgive their sin and heal their land."

God could forgive and heal the nation as He promised.

Afterwards, Katharina the English teacher invited Nancy and me to stay for a while. But I had to return to Edinburgh to resolve my financial situation and rent payments. The problem was, I didn't have a return ticket to home.

Katharina had been saving up in order to purchase a new car. She had managed to save enough to buy a car outright, but God spoke to her and exhorted her to defer the purchase. When she met me she felt God say, "The money is not for a car at the moment. Give three thousand Deutschmarks (the equivalent of one thousand five hundred dollar) to Emily!" This she did with a trusting heart.

This was an amazing financial provision from God. I contributed an offering to David as financial gift to put towards his living expenses as I had seen how little he had for himself, I then travelled back home.

There were only ten days left until the rent I owed on my apartment was due. I knew that I had to pay this overdue amount or face eviction. I had only a small amount of money and I needed much more than that amount to resolve the issue. The deadline loomed closer and I had no idea what to do. I prayed and trusted in God for His provision.

On June 30th, David telephoned me from Germany asking for my bank account number. I wondered about the reason for his asking for my account details as I believed that he could barely cover his own costs, let alone help someone else. I questioned him because I was convinced that he was in need himself.

But it came to light that he had been in part-time employment during his studies throughout the two years before he met me, because he wished to help with other's urgent financial needs. He had not spent any of his earnings but they had been deposited and saved in his bank account. He told me that he had had a dream on the night before he telephoned me, in which God directed him to give his savings to me. I was astonished at this unexpected phone call, not expecting that his offering would be able to settle my rent arrears. Nevertheless, I believed that this was God's provision.

Out of curiosity, I asked David how much he was planning to send me but he said to wait until I received it. So I gave him my bank account number, not knowing when and how much money would arrive. I was required to pay the amount I owed on the morning of July the 3rd. However, I still had no idea whether I would be able to pay the arrears. But God is always punctual! At 9am that day the money came through. The amount was exactly that which I needed to settle my overdue rent payment.

Many are the affliction of the righteous; But the Lord delivers him out of them all. (Psalm 34:19)

I immediately contacted the owner of my rented home and promised to pay the money that day. To my great relief, he accepted these terms. God had yet again performed another miracle!

I telephoned David to thank him, expressing my pain at having to receive his money as I was aware that he had given me all of his savings, which represented two years of hard work. However, he replied, "I am so happy because the money has gone to the place of God's choosing." I prayed for him over the telephone and asked God to bless him and give him numerous opportunities to travel to many nations just as the Lord had done for me.

Subsequently, every detail of David's dream has been fulfilled. We did in fact pray at the Sea of Galilee during a conference in Israel. He also came with me to a friend's wedding in Scotland. We did indeed fly business class to Korea although we had bought economy class tickets!

Since then, God has led David to the following countries: Israel, Egypt, England, Scotland, Wales, South Korea, Bangladesh, Thailand, Spain, Morocco, Bulgaria, Turkey, United States, Philippines, Uganda, Serbia and Belgium. My prayer for him had been answered! Not bad for a student whose only meal was once a little spaghetti and salt!

Do not withhold good from those to whom it is due, when it is in the power of your hand to do so. (Proverbs 3:27)

JEHOVAH ELYON—THE MOST HIGH

CHAPTER 4

The Fruits of Prayer

Call to Ukraine

GOD HAD HELPED ME SETTLE matters at home so I was released to go away on further ministry. I soon went back to join Nancy in Germany. Together we ministered to people who needed inner healing in Germany, Switzerland, France and Sweden over a period of one month. God arranged our entire schedule and so many people were blessed by our visits.

When Nancy and I were ministering in Sweden, we felt in our Spirit we must go to Ukraine for the next mission." Nancy had never heard of Ukraine before. She didn't even know that such a country existed! So we had to do some research and make some plans. It was important for this message of forgiveness for abuse to go further than we had initially envisaged. We finished our European ministry in Sweden, and we both flew from there to my home. Nancy spent some time with me, and then returned to her home in Houston, Texas.

Some months later, I had moved into temporary accommodation for a limited period. Because it was a stop-gap measure, no telephone line was supplied and I could not use the internet or fax for a few weeks. This made communication difficult. However, I was sure of one thing. God wanted Nancy and myself to go to Ukraine in mid-March! But neither of us had any contacts in Ukraine. This fact, coupled with my difficult home circumstances, made such a trip seem almost impossible. We needed a miracle that would produce a positive result, despite the negative circumstances. I had faith to believe that God had spoken, and therefore it would come to pass.

In God's providence, Pastor Berthold Klein of Germany supplied me with the telephone number and e-mail details of a pastor in Berlin who used to make regular trips to Ukraine. He kindly gave me the e-mail information I needed to contact a Ukrainian pastor, named Sergey, in the city of Vinnitsa.

I went to a friend's house in order to use his computer using internet to contact this person. So I sent off an e-mail explaining the reason for my intended visit.

Providentially again, the Ukrainian pastor's wife was an English teacher, so she could understand my e-mail and had no difficulty in communicating with me. Her name was Angelica.

When I went to enquire about travel to Ukraine, the travel agent said that in order to visit the country, we needed tourist visas. Before these could be made available to us we were required to be in possession of written confirmation of accommodation to show to the Ukrainian Embassy in London. Furthermore, we had to produce written evidence, so I contacted Angelica in Ukraine and she made the arrangements.

Angelica asked her church congregation whether anyone would be willing to accommodate Nancy and myself during our visit to her church. Several people responded and one young lady said that she had seen a vision of angels coming and she felt that we were being sent by God Himself. Because of this she was very keen to accommodate us and she offered to be our hostess while we were there.

A fee of thirty five pounds was required to be sent to the Ukrainian Embassy together with my passport, in order to obtain a tourist visa by post. But at that time, ten pounds was all I had.

However, if someone was able to personally visit the Embassy with my passport, it was permissible to pay a first instalment of ten pounds. The passport would then be officially stamped with the authorized tourist visa permission, and could be personally collected on payment of the remaining sum of twenty five pounds.

So I telephoned a friend in London and asked her to help by visiting the Ukrainian Embassy on my behalf. She was reluctant as she did not want to travel a long distance through the city. "What is the address of the Embassy?" she asked. I told her, and she responded happily. "That's the walking distance from my home!" So I sent my passport and the first instalment.

She went to the Embassy and was told that the process would take about a week. By that time I could send her the remaining amount. In due course, she collected my passport, officially stamped with a tourist visa for Ukraine, which she then posted on.

Being often short of money at this time tested and built my faith. I learnt obedience step by step and developed a total trust in the one true God, Who opens every door. I received my visa but still needed funds for a flight to Ukraine. I booked a ticket on a flight scheduled for the March 13th, but had no idea how God would provide for this expense.

There was a conference in Edinburgh from the 1st to the March 3rd, 2002. A famous American Christian author, Gene Edwards, came to preach. Gene had written more than thirty books including the most popular, 'A Tale of Three Kings.'

I attended this conference and there I met a Korean man who was the senior pastor of a large Korean Church in Boston Massachusetts, United States. He had wide experience in missionary outreach and had founded many churches in various countries.

Because I was the only Korean that he had come across at the conference, he was very interested to know the reason for God calling me to be a missionary to Scotland from Korea. After hearing some of my testimony, he wanted to know further details, so we arranged to meet the following day. I shared more of my story and told him about God's most recent call to go to Ukraine. There was so much to talk about and to share, that we decided to meet again.

At this meeting, the pastor asked about my current circumstances. I honestly felt that I had to admit that I was, at present, experiencing hardship. He then stated that he regarded my testimony as unique, and, speaking seriously, said, "I have never heard this kind of testimony although I've met so many missionaries and read many testimony books. You are the one true disciple among many I have met. You have not done anything on your own without the Holy Spirit's leading. Write a book! When you write the book in English I will translate it into Korean for you."

He then went on to say, "God has really touched my heart through your testimony and He has prompted me to pay for the ticket to Ukraine. I believe that God will do something amazing through your obedience to His call to minister in Ukraine." He said this as he handed me an envelope with the amount of money I needed to purchase my flight ticket! "God will bless you for obeying Him despite your difficult circumstances," he said.

Thanks be to God who sent a Korean pastor from Boston and supplied the flight ticket for the flight to Ukraine! I could never have imagined that, over three days, God would work in such an unexpected way, providing for the trip through this faithful pastor. This experience demonstrates yet again that God knows about all our needs and uses people from every nation who hear His voice to provide for those who obey His call. Jehovah Jireh was again proving his faithfulness in matters of provision. The Bible says for us to cast all our fear upon the Lord for he cares for us.

Nancy and I flew to Kiev, the capital of Ukraine on March 13th as pre-arranged. Because it was a five hour car journey from Kiev to Vinnitsa City, we had planned to take the train. I had mentioned this to Pastor Sergey on the telephone before we set off. However, when we arrived at Kiev Airport, Pastor Sergey and another brother had driven there to pick us up. We were very surprised when we saw a man holding a large placard bearing my name. I asked why they had gone to all that effort, when we could have just caught the train. They replied that they were so excited about meeting us that they wanted to see us as early as possible!

The next day was my birthday, and the pastor's family held a lovely banquet for me, even though we had never met before! The pastor's mother-in-law had come to his house to organize the event and cooked all kinds of local Ukrainian dishes. I experienced amazing warmth and love in the hearts of these believers. This family welcomed a stranger with a generous outpouring of kindness.

We are always at home in the company of those whose hearts are full of the love of Jesus! Christian people of all nationalities and backgrounds really do belong to one family.

Ukraine Mission

*W*ITHIN THE FIRST FEW DAYS of our trip, we attended an evening prayer meeting. The church congregation were all in attendance, about fifty people.

The meeting commenced with a man asking me about the number of countries I had visited. After several more questions, he suggested I give part of my testimony to the congregation, explaining how God had brought me to Ukraine. Nancy then also gave her testimony.

The people's hearts overflowed with the love of the Holy Spirit, and they arranged for us to share more over the next few days. I spoke about how hard it had been to make the trip to their particular church and of the obstacles that had been so difficult to overcome. The people were touched that God had brought sisters from so far away to specially minister to them and their hearts were open to our message.

One of these sessions at the church involved special teaching about the importance of holding a day and night of unceasing prayer and worship to God. Two figures from the Bible who inspire us in this are *Anna, who prayed and fasted for over sixty years before Jesus' first coming (Luke 2:37) and King David who organized and paid four thousand musicians and nearly three hundred singers to worship God both night and day. (1 Chronicle 23:1)*

The Full Gospel Church in Seoul, South Korea, also established the Prayer Mountain with night and day prayer. This was soon attracting over a million visitors per year, as people would spend retreats in the prayer cells provided on the mountain.

"On that day I will raise up the Tabernacle of David which

has fallen down, and repair its damage. I will raise up its ruins,
and build it as in the days of old." (Amos 9:11)

Nancy and I led some sessions of seminar about forgiveness
and intercession for a week. The congregation were so happy and
excited about our teaching.

The church where we were ministering did not normally
display floral arrangements, but one day a lady named Julia
brought three special flowers into the church and laid them near
the table at the front. There was one large beautiful yellow rose;
one purple orchid; and one other flower, white in color. Julia took
the microphone and addressed the people saying, "God showed
me these flowers in a vision, particularly the yellow rose with a
strong stem but there were no thorns on the rose and I sensed that
'This beautiful big yellow rose represents the outward beauty of
Emily and the strong stem depicts her inner strength of faith.'

Julia then went on to say, "I wanted to explain to Emily about
the vision, so I went to a flower shop, where I discovered this
magnificent yellow rose from which the thorns had already been
removed. I was amazed that the shop stocked roses with no thorns
which exactly fulfilled my vision. So I bought this rose and brought
it to explain what God had shown me. And also God directed me
to this passage from the Song of Solomon chapter six verse ten:
'Who is she who looks forth as the morning; Fair as the moon,
Clear as the sun, Awesome as an army with banners?' God gave
me this word for Emily."

After she finished speaking, the pianist stood up and declared:
"I also saw God's glory over Emily when she was sharing the Word
of God!"

These women encouraged me through sharing what God
had shown them. I felt valued by God and this meant so much
after I had obeyed by coming to Ukraine despite complex and
difficult circumstances. It would have been very easy to give up

on God's calling to minister in Ukraine but God blessed me for my obedience.

Nancy had an interesting experience while we were in Ukraine. She felt that she was constantly being prompted to buy a new purse! She did not want another purse and had no intention of spending the funds she had on something which was not needed. Her current purse was in excellent condition. However, the feeling did not go away, and in fact it grew stronger and stronger! Nancy finally gave in and purchased another purse on the way to dinner at the home of a young couple and their family from the church.

When we arrived at their home, we were very touched that this family had insisted on inviting us for a meal. They were obviously so very poor. It was, we discovered, the birthday of Julia, the young wife. Nancy had an idea for a gift and began to empty out her first purse asking Julia whether she had any use for a purse like that. Julia began to cry, and ran and found a picture of something that she had needed and been praying about for her birthday. It was a picture of Nancy's purse! God had wonderfully answered her prayer and Julia was overjoyed!

One night, at an intercessory prayer meeting, a woman stood up and asked us to pray for her brother. He had been an airline pilot. He was divorced from his wife, and was now suffering from cancer. He was in a terrible financial situation and had lost all his money and property. Because of the hopelessness of his condition, he had contemplated suicide.

After the meeting, when everyone had gone home, I felt that the pastor, his wife, Nancy and I should go to see the man the following morning and demonstrate God's care and compassion. We could not contact his sister to pre-arrange the visit because she had no telephone. However, we decided to visit him anyway.

When we arrived, the man's sister welcomed us at her door. Excitedly, she explained that God had spoken to her that morning and had told her, "Emily will come and pray for your brother today." She had told her brother, who was a non-believer, about God's message and when we arrived he was amazed that we should come to support him.

When we gathered to minister to the man, I asked the pastor to pray first, then his wife, followed by Nancy. After everyone else had prayed for him, I prayed and spoke with him having placed my hand on his heart. I explained some truths to him about Jesus.

I said "In this world, every person, from the richest and most successful in society to the poorest person, suffers. You are not alone in suffering. The only hope and solution is Jesus. In the Bible, Jesus says, *"I am the way, the truth and the life. No one comes to the Father except through Me."* When Jesus lives in you; you will have perfect peace and joy in your life. God sent us to this country especially to pray for you and share about His love."

I preached the gospel and after this he began to cry. "I remember all of what you have just shared with me and I accept these truths." he said. "Now I will go to a quiet place and pray to God." he whispered.

This man had experienced salvation for the first time when the Holy Spirit touched him. He was changed and had been lifted out of the desperation and depression. He now longed for more of the presence of God and wanted to spend time alone with his Savior.

At a later date, we had the privilege of visiting a hospital for the elderly. Pastor Sergey and his wife Angelica had links with the hospital and took us there to minister to the people. We prayed for individual patients, shared with them about Jesus and some were saved.

We shared the love of God with many people and God led us to intercede in many specific places. One of these was an underground storage chamber where Hitler had stockpiled weapons and explosives. We could not go underground, but had a time of prayer on the surface. We prayed for victims of the Holocaust and their families and also asked God for forgiveness for Ukraine's links with Hitler during World War Two.

When it was time for us to leave, the Ukrainian woman with whom we had been staying gave us a surprise farewell dinner. Her mother was so happy that we had come to stay with her daughter. She prepared many Ukrainian dishes, with the food all laid out on a big table. The leaders and other key people from the church were present to bid us farewell.

One little lady wanted to give us a parting gift to bless us but had nothing but a small piece of embroidered material that had belonged to her great grandmother. Before we left, she took it, cut it in half, and made two little bags, one for Nancy and one for me. She placed aromatic grass inside each one. We were deeply touched by her kind and loving gesture.

After the party was finished, Pastor Sergey knelt and asked Nancy and myself to pray for him. We did so and he was touched by Holy Spirit. His wife and many others queued to receive prayer as well. Nancy and I prayed and blessed each of them.

God had sent us to Ukraine with a purpose, and we completed our mission by listening to His guidance and obeying His will. After finishing everything God had shown us to do, we had a special farewell service at the church. It was very moving and each of the believers wept and hugged us as we sadly parted. We had come to know all fifty members of the church as our brothers and sisters in Christ.

God honored our obedience when we travelled to Ukraine to minister in His name. He used a Korean, an American and a Ukrainian as one family to bring blessing to others. It was an unforgettable time of sharing God's love, and was greatly anointed by the Lord. God works in unimaginable ways and orchestrates things perfectly to ensure His will is done.

Now to Him who is able to do exceedingly abundantly above all that we ask or think, according to the power that works in us (Ephesians 3:20)

JEHOVAH EL OLAM—THE EVERLASTING GOD

From Israel to Wedding Bells in Scotland

WHEN I WAS IN GERMANY again for inner healing ministry with Nancy, I visited David who had only a little spaghetti and salt when I visited first time. While I was at his home, there was a call for me from the secretary of a man, Tom Hess, in Israel. Mr Hess managed a day and night full-time prayer house in Israel and was the leader of the All Nations Convocation which was to be held in Israel a few months later. He made an earnest appeal for me to come and speak at the convocation as a representative of Scotland.

Tom had heard my testimony in Uganda and he sincerely wanted me to come to the Convocation.

The Convocation would be held over two weeks and involve supporters of Israel together with many intercessors. Two hundred countries would be represented. But when the secretary informed me of the actual dates of, I had to decline. I could not attend because there was a clash with my friend Jane's wedding in Edinburgh. I had promised Jane to attend her wedding. It was very important to me that I be present, as Jane was a very special friend who had been coming to the prayer meeting in my house for some years.

Jane had a beautiful unselfish nature and generously supported me and many people in various ways. Because I valued her friendship so highly, I wanted to be present at her wedding to bless and pray for her.

David overheard my telephone conversation with the secretary in Israel. As he was soon to graduate from his theological college, he mentioned enthusiastically that the first place he wanted to visit after graduation was Israel! Now my mind was in turmoil! Should I accept the invitation to the Convocation in Israel and take David there, or should I keep my promise to Jane and attend her wedding in Edinburgh?

After discussing this with Jane, she insisted that I must go with David to Israel. So I did, but there was still no peace in my mind about missing Jane's wedding.

David had given me a monetary gift to spend in whichever way I wished. I shared my dilemma with David in Israel and he said that I could use the funds to help pay for flights to attend the wedding. I recalled that two years before David had met me; he had dreamed that he would be attending a wedding in Scotland. I decided to fly with him to Jane's wedding for two days at the weekend, in the middle of the conference. I made this decision in obedience to the dream he had had previously and because the cost of our flight tickets was exactly the amount David had brought. I felt that this was God's leading and His provision.

When we did travel back in the middle of the Convocation to attend the wedding, we experienced some difficulties and obstacles. The airport officials in Israel interrogated us separately for about two hours. They were suspicious of us leaving in the middle of the conference and because the 9/11 terror attack had recently occurred, security services were on high alert!

Nonetheless, I was determined to travel at this time. No matter the cost or how difficult it might be to get there. We almost missed our flight but eventually landed in time to attend the wedding.

I had met Jane's fiancé, James, when she had brought him to the prayer meetings in my home. Their wedding was a very special and blessed event and I was extremely pleased to be part of it. I felt that the journey had been worth the effort to attend and David enjoyed it immensely too. Every aspect of the wedding was exactly as he had seen in his prophetic dream years earlier!

During their married life Jane and James demonstrated their

love towards others many times. Their kindness was Christ-like. They cared about needy people and still do.

After the wedding, David and I returned to the Convocation in Israel. Despite the 9/11 tragedy, about a thousand brave intercessors from all over the world came to pray and support Israel.

The focus of the conference on the day that we returned was "Europe" so I was asked to report on Scotland to all the people who were gathered. When I came down from the platform after finishing speaking, I was approached by a lady called Carole Brown from North Carolina, in the United States. She had been listening in the crowd as I spoke. Carole handed me a personal note with a message which she believed God had given her. This is what she had written: "God's love is full in your heart. Your prayers touch the throne of God. Go directly to God, because He births prayer in you."

After God had spoken to her, she wanted to get to know me better. She felt God impress upon her heart that I was special in His eyes. So I shared more with her about what He had done in my life and we had fellowship together. After hearing some of my testimony she said: "You should write a book. But get it published in the United States."

Carole invited me to America and sometime later I visited her beautiful home in North Carolina during which time we developed a close friendship. This was one of the relationships that God established for me during the conference. Also, while at the Convocation in Jerusalem, I met other precious people, more divine connections.

One of these people was Rosemary Schindler, a relative of Oskar Schindler, immortalized in the film "Schindler's List." Rosemary lived in Oakland California U.S.A and her life was devoted to caring for Jewish people. God had revealed this special calling to her whilst she had visited Israel some years earlier. One morning, she had been praying on the Mount of Olives when she received a revelation from God, convincing her that the Lord wanted her to express His unconditional love to His people. She then devoted her time and energy to fulfilling this calling.

In a newspaper interview Rosemary once declared: "The world needs to hear this message: Oskar was willing to lay down his life for his friends and give everything he had for their salvation." It was such a joy for me to meet Rosemary and learn more of God's heart for Jewish people! The Bible encourages us to,

Pray for the peace of Jerusalem: may they prosper who love you. (Psalm 122:6)

Rosemary also invited me to her home in Oakland California and I had a wonderful Easter holiday with her sometime later. I am so grateful to God who gave me so many wonderful blessings and divine appointments in Israel. Since then, Rosemary has visited me four times for an intercessory ministry for Scotland. We have visited Korea twice together to speak in churches, led by the Holy Spirit.

I was blessed by the divine connections God had ordained for me during the conference and am so grateful to God who gave me so many wonderful blessings.

I have trusted God and obeyed His direction for my life. This has led me to travel to different countries and there I have met many other servants of Christ who have responded to His voice. In this way, while obeying each step of His plan, I in turn, received the resources I needed to continue in obedience. Trusting God is always the right way to live, as He always provides the wherewithal to carry out His will. Each event was a perfectly fitting piece of God's mosaic of miracles in my life!

Trust in the Lord with all your heart and lean not on your own understanding. In all your ways acknowledge Him and He will direct your paths. (Proverbs 3:5-6)

Jane and James's wedding

Emily Chang, Rosemary Schindler and Pastor Youngtae Lim

God Meets My Precise Needs

ALSO MADE ANOTHER CONNECTION, MY friend Esther, whom I had met earlier at the Convocation in Israel. She visited my home in Scotland to pray for the country, and during her visit, we formed a strong friendship as we shared our experiences of God.

Esther invited me to her home in California and I explained that I would be going to Los Angeles soon to care for my niece as she awaited the birth of her baby. I promised Esther that I would visit, and later that year, when I arrived in Los Angeles, I called her. She told me that she would still love to welcome me to her home. I explained that I could only come for two days because I needed to support my niece and her newborn baby. She felt this would be too short and encouraged me to come for at least a week. I turned down her offer due to my family commitment, so she offered to come with some friends and see us in Los Angeles, traveling six hours by car! She wanted her friends to hear my testimony, as she knew it was powerful and encouraging.

When they arrived, we ate, chatted and shared God's love. By bringing these guests to my niece's home the Lord performed an unforgettable miracle for me. It was the most overwhelming miracle of provision that I had experienced in my life as a Christian!

At this time, I desperately and urgently needed about ten thousand dollars to meet my many financial commitments which were related to my children's education costs. So I prayed earnestly about this matter, and God gave me a deep peace, although I had no idea where the money would come from! I simply prayed to God asking for him to provide as he had done for me in the past. I asked for the exact amount needed, ten thousand dollars! I trusted God and left the matter in His hands.

After Esther, her friends and I had shared time together; we all went to bed at three in the morning, following our lengthy time of fellowship. We went to our separate rooms to try and get some sleep.

As I lay down in my bed, Esther came to my room a short time after we had all said goodnight. She was holding her check book and said, "I will give you a check. You tell me the amount."

I was bewildered by her action of coming into my room and offering me money as I had not mentioned or even hinted to her, that I needed financial help at this time. Also, I had the impression that she was an ordinary person, with a modest income as she had told me that she did not work. Because of this, I guessed that she might be able to give me a modest amount, so I asked her to write only the maximum that she could afford. She refused and asked me to state the amount that was needed. I felt what I needed was a huge sum, so I kept refusing repeatedly but she pressed me to tell her.

She explained that she had been trying to sleep, when the Holy Spirit told her clearly to give me a check and indicated a precise amount that He wanted her to give me. She asked me to tell her the amount that I needed as she wanted to confirm in her own mind that she had heard God correctly. In view of her reply I became confident and full of assurance that God was answering my prayer. So I told her the amount for which I had prayed, ten thousand dollars!

"Exactly!" exclaimed Esther joyfully and immediately wrote the check for ten thousand dollars and signed it! I marveled. I needed to confirm for myself that God was definitely leading her to provide the money that I had asked Him for repeatedly in prayer. So I questioned her, "When you came to Los Angeles to see me, did you intend to give me a financial offering?" She said that she had not had that intention and explained, "The Holy Spirit told me only just now, while I was trying to sleep."

I was not aware of Esther's family situation, so in order to avoid any misunderstanding between herself and her husband regarding her gift to me, I asked her to check with her husband that it was all right with him also. She did so and her husband was happy to give his agreement.

Esther demonstrated through this gift, her amazing generosity and willingness to obey God's commands. She was used by God to show His amazing care for my needs. God had heard my prayers and was very particular in His provision for the exact amount that my family and I required at that time.

After Esther had given me the miraculous check, I could not sleep from excitement as I thought of what God had done! I rejoiced in His deep care for me. I was able to obtain the necessary funds for the educational fees I had to pay on the exact date when they were required.

God is in sovereign control of every detail of my life; and He has the same lavish love and compassion for all His people. *Call upon Me in the day of trouble; I will deliver you, and you shall glorify Me. (Psalm 50:15)*

Esther offered to hold a celebration for my Jubilee fiftieth birthday in her city. She invited some of my American friends, along with her own, to join us. To my amazement, she took us to a high-class restaurant for a special party with a beautifully decorated birthday cake. She generously covered all the costs and such care and love illustrated again her warm and generous disposition. Furthermore, Esther surprised me with many lovely gifts. I felt God's presence through the whole event, and He seemed to be rewarding my service to Him by using her generosity! To God be all the glory!

The Lord moved upon Esther's heart and she continued to bless me in many other ways. I am so grateful to her and to God, who brought us together as sisters in Christ. When God brings people together, beautiful relationships form and they are blessings to each other.

"By this everyone will know that you are my disciples, if you love one another." (John 13:35)

I have to add another story to show the way in which God met my precise needs. God has shown His provision for me in so many different ways. Another example was when He blessed me with a series of expensive dental treatments. I required surgery and many implants for which God met my needs in an amazing way!

A Korean couple, who were both Christian dentists, was staying for a year in London where the wife was completing advanced studies in dentistry. I first met them through a friend, who also lived in London. The husband, named Soonho Jung was a specialist in dental implants, and his wife's expertise was in fitting braces. The family wanted to spend some time in Edinburgh but I had to be in London at that time. So I gave them the keys to my home so they could stay and enjoy their holiday there. In gratitude for providing accommodation for his family, Dr. Soonho kindly offered me a complimentary dental check-up and treatment the next time I was in Korea.

Later, Dr. Soonho went back to Korea and his wife stayed on for further studies in London. When I went to Korea I didn't go to his dental clinic because I had only met him once. I knew my procedures would be very expensive, as I had to get several dental implants.

A few months later, his wife, Dr. Yeonjin, needed to take an examination at Edinburgh University on completion of her studies, so she came to stay with me. Dr. Yeonjin left London in such a hurry that she forgot to bring several important personal items. I was able to provide the items she needed, but the biggest problem was that she forgot her computer power charger.

Dr. Yeonjin arrived on a Sunday evening and all the stores were closed. Her examination was the next morning, and using the little power left in her laptop computer, we managed to transfer all her study material from her laptop to my laptop. Using my laptop, she studied all through the night in preparation for her examination. She was grateful for my assistance and wanted to bless me by offering a dental examination from which she ascertained that I urgently needed dental treatment. She suggested that I go to Korea as soon as possible to see her husband who would perform the needed dentistry at minimal cost.

Consequently, I went to Korea for my dental treatment which required four implants and a bone operation at the estimated cost of twelve thousand dollars. Dr. Soonho graciously charged me only two thousand dollars and I agreed to have the treatment. I knew I needed it urgently and I was also grateful that it was being offered to me at such a good price.

However, despite the generous discount, I could not even afford that minimum charge. When I contacted a friend in order to discuss this matter, the friend willingly offered to lend that amount of money. I assured the lender that God would give back the money before I left Korea.

After the treatment, I began to pray that God would provide. However, even after my arrival at the airport, to return to Edinburgh, God did not provide me with the money, so I started to get anxious. Whilst waiting in the airport for my flight home, I received an unexpected call from a friend who asked me if I had a Korean bank account. I told her that I did, and she explained that she got the some extra income that month and the Holy Spirit had given her a very clear direction that she should give me the sum of money that would cover my treatments!

At first, she had resisted the voice of the Holy Spirit because she wanted to use it for other purposes. But, God showed her that He was relying on her and had reminded her afresh that He wanted her to give this amount to me. For this reason, she had called me and offered to transfer the amount immediately! I had never imagined that this person would call and offer the exact amount to meet my needs!

This was another example of God's miraculous care. Just one

hour before I flew out of Korea, God provided the money in exactly the way I had asked. It was wonderful to telephone my friend who had initially covered those dental costs and share the testimony of how God had provided yet again and I could pay back to my friend before I left Korea.

Faith is the substance of things hoped for, the evidence of things not seen. (Hebrews 11; 1)

Living by faith is sometimes not easy in the natural realm: but it is challenging and exciting because we discover that God cares for us and He never lets us down. When we trust totally in Him the Lord always miraculously meets our needs in His way.

Dr Yeonjin Ko

Dr Soonho Jung

Swiss Mission

*T*HE LORD DIRECTED MY FRIEND Geraldine and me to travel across Switzerland, starting from Geneva, then continuing through Lausanne, Bern, Lucerne and Zurich to intercede for these cities in June 2003. So we went to Switzerland for a week. My only Swiss friends were in Basel where I had ministered previously, but we had no contacts in Geneva. So we obeyed God and travelled first to Geneva.

When we arrived, I called a pastor known to me in Basel. He gave me the telephone number of a pastor in Geneva, but he could not speak any English because Geneva is a French speaking city. So I spoke to the pastor in Basel and he translated for the pastor in Geneva, explaining the purpose of our visit.

Geraldine and I caught a train to central Geneva, and the pastor met us at the station as we had arranged. He took us to his home and provided us with excellent hospitality, but because of the language barrier, he called on the services of an interpreter.

The pastor and his wife were glad of our visit so he invited us to join the intercessory prayer meeting which took place an hour before the Sunday service. We prayed that morning and joined people for the service. The believers there were greatly encouraged and we enjoyed the fellowship with them.

The next stage of our journey was Lausanne. Our interpreter told us that there were many Koreans there and offered to drive us in her car. We met about forty Korean students at the Youth with a Mission Centre.

After lunch, the leader of YWAM in Lausanne gave me helpful information which would later allow my son to join the YWAM Discipleship Training School!

Geraldine and I then traveled to Bern where we met a person

who had been contacted by our Genevan pastor friend and who was willing to offer us hospitality. We praised God for His generous provision for His people.

During this time, we went to the highest area of parkland in Bern where we interceded and prayed over the city outstretched below us. We went next to Lucerne for a short time of prayer and then onto Zurich where I knew a couple who were prayer leaders. We stayed two nights in their Zurich prayer house beside the lake with its beautiful unrestricted view. We all prayed for Zurich together and the couple who were hosting us in the house was very kind and hospitable. They showed us around beautiful parts of the city and treated us generously, taking us out for dinner and giving kind gifts to remember them by.

A Swiss woman from another prayer house came to visit us, having heard that two intercessors had arrived from Scotland. She told us that the following day, forty Swiss prayer warriors would be meeting together to launch intercessory prayer for their parliament in Bern, the capital of Switzerland. They invited us to attend the meeting. Geraldine and I had now been joined by two Brazilians, and our group was permitted to merge with the intercession team praying for Switzerland's Parliament. The Brazilian lady and her son had been praying for Switzerland for many years in Brazil, but God had directed her to go and intercede in Switzerland this particular week!

On the day of the prayer meeting for the parliament, we were also asked by a Swiss intercessor, "Why have you both come to Switzerland?" I explained that God had directed us to come to intercede for the Swiss nation as well.

Three Christian Members of Parliament initiated this event of prayer for the forty Swiss intercessors who were invited to tour the parliament buildings. After that, we were taken to the roof top of the building where we spent time praying for the government and the nation of Switzerland. While on that roof top, a man asked the group, "Why are we not seeing any fruit in Switzerland?"

I replied by drawing his attention to the words of Jesus in the gospel of John, Chapter 12:24-25 which states *"Truly, truly, I say to you unless a grain of wheat falls into the earth and dies, it remains by itself alone, but if it dies, it bears much fruit. He who loves his life loses it, and he who hates his life in this world shall keep it to life eternal."*

I explained that the death of selfishness and the sacrifice of prayer would bring fruit. Also, following Jesus as His disciples would bring the harvest they desired to see in Switzerland.

The Swiss Christians were greatly encouraged by the fact that God had sent intercessors from Scotland and Brazil to share fellowship with them in prayer at this particular time. They realized that God had not forgotten Switzerland because He manifested His love for their country by sending people to support them in prayer. They testified to God's kindness and care demonstrated through our concern for them. This mission was unique in the sense that by simply being there, we were used in the purpose of God for Switzerland.

JEHOVAH SHAMMAH—
THE LORD WHO IS PRESENT

Geraldine, Emily and a Brazilian lady

CHAPTER 5

And it Shall be Called a House of Prayer

ONE DAY, I WAS SPEAKING on the telephone to Sangsook, my best friend in Korea.

During our conversation, Sangsook felt the Holy Spirit say that I should meet Jean Darnall, the Youth with a Mission lecturer who is also a pastor and a prophetess. The thing was, neither of us knew where she lived.

The following day, I was attending a prayer meeting in Edinburgh dedicated to praying for the government of Scotland. At this meeting, there was a YWAM mission group of fourteen people from California. Among them, a lady named Fawn Parish gave me a copy of her book 'All about You Jesus' as well as a DVD interviewing Jean Darnall. I exclaimed when she handed me the DVD, "Only yesterday my friend felt that I must meet her, but we didn't know where Jean Darnall lived, or how to contact her."

Fawn Parish said she worked alongside Jean Darnall who lived close by in Los Angeles! This was obviously a divine appointment arranged by God.

Soon after, I had the opportunity to travel to Los Angeles where I met Jean Darnall during a prayer meeting entitled 'Pray for LA.' Most of the people were from 'The Church on the Way' where Pastor Jack Hayford ministered.

After the meeting, Jean Darnall prophesied over me without knowing anything saying, "Those who support and help you, God will not forget any of them. He will remember them all and He will bless each one. Through your book, your ministry will be enlarged and God will open up opportunities in radio and TV broadcasts. Your place will be enlarged. You have been on the narrow way where most people don't want to go. Your prayer is not in vain and your work is not in vain. Your ministry is flexible and adaptable, a move around ministry which God gave to you. Go wherever God wants you to go, and be wherever God wants you to be."

Then Jean said, "I just saw a very big house with many rooms. Did God give you this?" "Not yet, but He will" I replied. She said "Claim it!"

I knew in my heart that this house was to be the House of Prayer and Worship in Scotland. God had shown me many times previously that He would give me a prayer house in Scotland like the Tabernacle of David in the Scripture. God spoke to me through His servant Jean Darnall, confirming this promise of the prayer House in Scotland.

In Korea there are more than five hundred Prayer Mountains where people come to stay in the accommodation provided.

Constant prayer and intercession arises to God twenty four hours a day, seven days a week.

In Amos 9:11 the Bible says, *"On that day I will raise up the Tabernacle of David which has fallen down, and repair its damages. I will raise up its ruins, and rebuild it as in the days of old."*

In Europe, there is a sad lack of intensive prayer and very few are committed to such sacrificial prayer times. Nevertheless, in European countries, there are Prayer Houses where people meet with God and intercede for their nation. The Lord showed me that He wanted a Prayer House in Scotland where He would bring intercessors from many different countries to pray for all nations throughout the day and night.

I am convinced that God will soon provide a house for unceasing prayer and thereby demonstrate, yet again, His inexhaustible ability to answer prayer and perform miracles!

My faith that this is God's intention has increased because I was given a very special and detailed confirmation through a group of eight young Korean Christians whom God sent in the summer of 2011 to intercede for Scotland.

They came from a church in Korea where young people are sent out on mission trips during their summer and winter vacations. God directed them to go to Edinburgh. They were so surprised and wondered what God had planned for them in Scotland. They asked God whom they were to meet in Edinburgh, praying and requesting that the Holy Spirit give them direction. By divine connection, they were able to find my details. They contacted me and I invited them to stay at my home for a week.

Led by the Holy Spirit, we ministered to people who needed prayer and interceded for the city. We spent one entire day specifically praying for God to establish the Prayer House that had been promised many times. Two group members received an identical vision, including architectural details from the Holy Spirit. Their drawings of the house were from an external and internal perspective and both were exactly the same! One of them said, "I received this from the Lord's guidance as though He was holding my hand as these designs were being drawn."

"All this," said David in the Bible, *"The Lord made me understand in writing, by His hand upon me, all the works of these plans." (1 Chronicles 28:19)*

We were all amazed that God had given two people such detailed and identical visions just as God showed David a vision of the architectural plan of Solomon's Temple. We were reminded of the story of Noah in Genesis, Chapter six, when God gave Noah specific instructions to build an ark.

And this is how you shall make it: The length of the ark shall be 300 cubits, its width 50 cubits and its height 30 cubits. You shall make a window for the ark and you shall finish it to a cubit from above and set the door of the ark in its side. You shall make it with lower, second and third decks. (Genesis 6:15-16)

We were also reminded of Moses in Exodus where God gives clear and detailed directions on how to build the Tabernacle.

Moreover, you shall make the Tabernacle with ten curtains of fine woven linen and blue, purple and scarlet thread; with artistic designs of cherubim you shall weave them. The length of each curtain shall be twenty-eight cubits and the width of each curtain four cubits. And every one of the curtains shall have the same measurements. (Exodus 26:1-2)

God also gave us the location of the Prayer House through the same two people who had drawn exactly the same pictures of how the house appeared in their visions. They made me a large scale drawing of the details of the prayer house. It currently hangs in my room as an enormous encouragement and motivation to pray for this to be revealed soon.

God has performed so many miracles in my life as described in this book, and I am certain that He will establish the prayer house as He has confirmed so many times already.

When I was born again on that wonderful day years before, I did not have any idea of my destiny and the purpose God had for my life. He is still leading me on the pathway of His will, and I am so happy to be obedient and to follow Him.

Throughout my journey with God, the Lord has also blessed my children. During all my mission trips, He always provided someone to look after them while they were still young. God has been faithful, sending them to prestigious schools and universities and calling one to become a licensed lawyer in Washington DC.

To God be all the Glory for His grace and power in my life.

Be exalted, O God, above the heavens; Let Your glory be above all the earth. (Psalm 57:5)

Be exalted, O Lord, in Your own strength! We will sing and praise Your power. (Psalm 21:13)

Let the people praise You, O God; Let all the peoples praise You. Oh, let the nations be glad and sing for joy! For you shall judge the people righteously, And govern the nations on earth. Selah Let the peoples praise You, O God; let all the peoples praise You. (Psalm 67:3-5)

I will sing to the Lord as long as I live; I will sing praise to my God while I have my being. (Psalm 104:33)

The Weaver

My Life is but a weaving
between my Lord and me;
I cannot choose the colours
He worketh steadily.

Oft times He weaveth sorrow
And I, in foolish pride,
Forget He sees the upper,
And I the underside.

Not till the loom is silent
And the shuttles cease to fly,
Shall God unroll the canvas
And explain the reason why.

The dark threads are as needful
In the Weaver's skilful hand,
As the threads of gold and silver
In the pattern He has planned.

He knows, He loves, He cares,
Nothing this truth can dim.
He gives His very best to those
Who leave the choice with Him.

Author-unknown

This poem shows that there is a divine purpose involved in everything that God plans or permits in our lives. The same principle applies to the mosaic of my own life. God takes the various pieces represented by the experiences of my life, and He fits them together within the mystery of His own will, to produce the pattern of His choice.

At times He allows suffering and frustration. At other times He brings us a challenge, seeking from us the response of faith and obedience. From these pieces of our life God in His grace, makes the mosaic that He has chosen. This process continues for a life-time. God is a God of perfection. He can never be satisfied with anything sub-standard.

The mosaic of my life will not be finished until God is pleased with His own handiwork. The Lord Himself is able to achieve this result and I have the reassuring truth of His word to give me peace and joy:

Blessed are all those who put their trust in Him (Psalm 2:12)

NEVER COMPLAIN TO GOD AND GIVE
THANKS IN ALL CIRCUMSTANCES, CLING
TO GOD WHEN YOU ARE IN A TRIAL

Emily Chang
blessingallnations@hotmail.co.uk

(Some of the personal names that appear in this book have been changed in order to protect the privacy of the individuals.)